The Challenge
of Coexistence

Hugh Gaitskell

HARVARD UNIVERSITY PRESS
CAMBRIDGE

1957

Library of Congress Catalog Card Number: 57–9075
Printed in the United States of America

The Godkin Lectures on the Essentials of Free Government and the Duties of the Citizen were established at Harvard University in memory of Edwin Lawrence Godkin (1831–1902).

Foreword

These lectures had to be delivered at a time of exceptional uncertainty in world affairs. Suez and Hungary had exploded, but the smoke had not cleared away. It was difficult to foresee all their consequences or to guess what new eruptions were likely in the already disturbed international scene. There was a greater danger than ever that anything said might quickly be rendered out of date by the swift march of events.

I thought of trying to avoid this danger by keeping the discussion on a high philosophical plane. But I soon dropped the idea, since I had neither the qualities nor the time required. Moreover, to have talked about the "Challenge of Coexistence" without referring directly or indirectly to the sensational events of last fall would have been absurd. I decided that I preferred the risk of appearing out of date to possible future readers to the certainty of being dull to the audience at Harvard!

Although I gave only three lectures, I could not have managed to prepare them during and after the intense political activity of last summer and fall without the assistance of several people. In particular, I wish to thank my three Parliamentary colleagues, Mr. Philip Noel-Baker, Mr. Kenneth Younger, and Mr. Denis Healey, whose advice was invaluable, and my wife, without whose help in many different ways I should never have been able to finish the final version in time.

The lectures published here are substantially as delivered except that at one or two points I have added some explanatory sentences and at one or two others I have, I hope, slightly improved the grammar!

H. G.

Contents

Contents

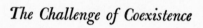

The Challenge of Coexistence

I

Coexistence and the United Nations

I̲T IS so great an honor to be invited to deliver these lectures that in trying to prepare them during these last weeks, I have felt an increasing sense of diffidence. For professional politicians, when they have been in the job for any length of time, are not well fitted for really deep thinking, partly because they have no time for it and partly because the very practice of their art involves them in continual simplification. If the expert is a man who knows more and more about less and less, the politician is a man who knows less and less about more and more! The superficial is always attractive to a politician because it is so easily communicated, whereas if he tries to be profound, he will either be misunderstood or merely regarded as a bore.

Nor can I claim that in my case these intellectual handicaps are balanced by recent practical experience in government. For, unfortunately, it is over five years since I was a member of any government. And the experience one gathers in opposition is of a limited kind. One is certainly close to the government. But the angle from which one observes it is very special.

Some of you may feel that the title "The Challenge of Coexistence" is not quite so appropriate after Hungary and Suez. These events certainly have a very direct bearing both on the nature of the challenge and the answers to be given to it. But I do not think this would justify abandoning it as a title. Let me, however, interpolate that it is not my intention, despite recent events, to alter its significance so far as to make it mean *just* the problem of coexistence between the United States and Britain!

Few things are more boring than trying to arrive at precise definitions. But I cannot really embark upon these lectures without saying something about the word "coexistence." Most people today think of it as a Russian slogan — rather blown upon by their latest behavior. It is a Russian slogan. But it was not Khrushchev or even Stalin, but Lenin, who first introduced the term. He used it to describe periods during which Soviet policy would abandon the all-out attack on every front against the noncommunist world and replace it by the more subtle tactics of concluding agreements with some governments and in some areas, while keeping up intense pressure elsewhere.

The purpose of coexistence, according to Lenin, was purely tactical and the phase strictly temporary. By changing the nature of the attack and relaxing the pressure, divisions in capitalist states, which were always inherent, would be allowed to develop and thus weaken the enemies of communism. The background to this idea was the familiar wholehearted belief in the ultimate collapse of capitalism, which it was the job of the true communist to hasten along, and the conviction that sooner or later a clash — an armed clash — between the communist and capitalist worlds could not be avoided.

There is no reason to doubt that, when the term was reintroduced by the Soviet leaders a few years ago, it had substantially the same significance for them as in Lenin's teaching. It was a change in the character of the cold war, a cold war which had in these years been conducted crudely and equally aggressively everywhere, in Asia, in India and Burma, for instance, against noncommunist governments there as it was against noncommunist governments in Europe.

The new phase of coexistence foreshadowed by Stalin before his death and developed by Malenkov and Khrushchev afterwards meant specifically, first, an acceptance of the *status quo* in Europe. Russia appeared for the time being to give up any intention of pushing out her frontiers in that continent, though no doubt she still retained some hope of detaching Germany from the West. On the other hand, she gave no sign that she was willing to withdraw her frontiers. She still appeared determined to keep her hold over all the satellite states. At the same time there was a slight lifting of the Iron Curtain. Cultural and technical exchange visits were encouraged, as long as they were strictly under control. Much friendlier language was used. There was a greater willingness to trade. Messrs. Bulganin and Khrushchev began their famous series of journeys.

Secondly, the new coexistence involved a change in policy toward the governments of the so-called uncommitted areas. Great efforts were made to cultivate friendly relations with them in place of the earlier policy of attempting to upset them by internal communist activity. Indeed, the chief nature of the change was to let the European front quiet down, while developing, principally through more subtle propaganda, trade, and other nonwarlike means, the cold war in these uncommitted areas.

A number of agreements were concluded which illustrate the change in the policy. They involved very little cost to the Soviets and secured for them considerable gains in good will. The Korean armistice was at last signed. A treaty was concluded with the

West about Austria, and Soviet troops were withdrawn. A base was returned to Finland. More important, an agreement was concluded at Geneva regarding Indo-China. This agreement to divide the country, and later their willingness not to insist on general elections as originally provided for under the Geneva agreement, can be regarded as a concession by Ho Chi Min and by the Chinese, against which they no doubt counted the importance of the good will of India. Finally, special efforts were made to rebuild friendly relations with Yugoslavia, even to the extent of Canossa-like pilgrimages by the Soviet leaders to Marshal Tito.

Why did the Russians change their tactics? For three reasons, above all. First, it was clear that the tough policy had failed. They had made no advances in Europe. The democracies had been galvanized into a greater unity through NATO and more serious defense preparations. It was hoped, not without reason, that more subtle tactics would undermine this unity and the growing military strength of the West.

Secondly, there was a realization in Moscow of the increasing importance of the uncommitted states of the world, particularly India. These states had not achieved their independence when the tough cold war period began. But by 1952 it was clear that they had surmounted any immediate transitional difficulties and were certain to play a more and more significant part in world affairs.

Thirdly, while there was no sign that the Soviet leaders had abandoned their fundamental faith in world communism, there was a growing understanding that the nuclear stalemate might rule out the ultimate armed clash between capitalism and communism. Whatever public statements the Russian leaders made from time to time, in their hearts they must have realized that a third world war, fought with thermonuclear weapons, was bound to involve the destruction not only of capitalism, but of communism also.

While these were the reasons for the change, something else has clearly been happening behind the Iron Curtain which bears upon the application of this new tactic and is of great importance in itself. Both in the satellite countries and in Russia movements of opinion have begun to show themselves which may conceivably lead to a real departure from the rigid communist doctrine on foreign policy, which has hitherto, through all tactical changes, dominated the outlook of the Soviet government. What has happened in the last year, and particularly in the last few months, has, of course, carried this particular process very much further than most people foresaw three years ago.

I have not the qualifications nor the time to discuss in any detail the fascinating question of how and why this particular change has come about. Clearly the denunciation of Stalin by Khrushchev must have had a positively traumatic effect on Communist Party members everywhere. Then the weakening of the power of the secret police, no doubt necessary as "collective leadership" replaced "the cult of the individual" in Moscow, also weakened the power of the puppet governments in the satellite states. Again, both in those countries and in Russia the release of millions of political prisoners must have increased criticism of the regime. In the satellite states very bad economic conditions, the result of sheer exploitation by Russia, combined with intense nationalist feeling, played a big part. In Russia itself the huge expansion of technical education necessarily meant teaching people to think more for themselves. But thoughts about science may also have led to thoughts about politics. At the same time, the new managerial and professional class, conscious of its power and importance, seems to have been demanding better conditions, including more freedom of thought and speech. Even the slight lifting of the Iron Curtain has probably encouraged the process, too. That all these and no doubt other forces have been at work producing some kind of ferment is not now in question, though it is still too early to predict just what the consequences may be for the problem of coexistence.

Meanwhile, other countries have also been formulating their views on the subject. By far the most important statement has come not from the West but from the East, in the ten principles of the Bandoeng Conference. These principles may be regarded as just pious aspirations, but the fact that they are now the declared aspirations of most of the countries of Asia and Africa is itself not without significance. Apart from the endorsement of the Charter of the United Nations, their most important features are (1) the emphasis on equality "of small nations as well as large," (2) their dislike of "blocs," and an implied neutralism, and (3) anticolonialism.

Whatever we may think of them, the Bandoeng principles are certainly not communist. The coexistence which they imply is far more genuine than that of the Russians. The anticolonialism was aimed against Russia as well as against the West. Indeed, most of us would find it hard to quarrel with the principles, though we might feel that they did not take the danger of aggression sufficiently seriously. We might also wish to underline that for us coexistence could never be taken to mean contentment with a state of affairs in which peoples were not free and nations not independent everywhere.

To us, then, the challenge of coexistence is not merely how to avoid a third world war, not merely how to settle international disputes peacefully, to live and let live, not merely how to conduct an ideological struggle against totalitarian communism, but how to do these things and also to bring to those peoples who do not now enjoy them the benefits of liberty and true self-government.

So much for this rather lengthy introduction, the background to all three lectures. Now let me tell you how I propose to proceed. With three lectures to give, it is clearly convenient to pick out within the general framework three subjects which I can examine in detail. Happily, there is no great difficulty. There are, I suggest, three obvious spheres in which this problem of coexistence confronts us today.

First, there is the problem of the international institutions, in particular the United Nations. Just what part should it play in our policies? I propose to devote the rest of this first lecture to that question. Then there is the regional problem which arises where the most direct contact between the West and the communist bloc exists — the regional problem of Europe. I shall deal with this in my second lecture. Thirdly, there is the other major regional problem, the problem of the relationship and struggle with communism in the uncommitted areas — in Africa, Asia, and the Middle East. I shall come to this in my third lecture.

Let me turn, then, to the United Nations. Recent events have led to much questioning and criticism of the United Nations in Britain. People who hitherto did not know much about it, or perhaps took it for granted as "a good thing," are now beginning to wonder. They are also, I believe, rather confused. One can distinguish two extreme points of view. There are those who look upon the United Nations as a kind of organization or institution apart, which is expected to deal with anything in the world that is thrust upon it. Their attitude toward it is rather like their attitude toward their own government. If they think something is wrong at home they expect their government to deal with it; similarly, if there is trouble abroad they expect the United Nations as an outside authority to handle it.

At the opposite extreme there are those who regard the United Nations as a useless and even harmful talking shop, which delays and hampers governments and even prevents them from acting decisively and positively on their own in what they conceive to be either their own interests or those of the world as a whole. And, of course, most governments in most countries have no difficulty in identifying these two objectives.

While these attitudes to the United Nations are normally found among very different people, they are sometimes also combined in the same person. In recent weeks a number of my countrymen have taken the first line about Hungary and the second about Suez. Indeed, where the problem is an awkward one, which a national government does not wish to deal with because it is too dangerous and there is no easy solution, then people are inclined to say, "Of course, the United Nations should deal with it." If, on the other hand, the problem is one in which a national government believes that it can, by using its own power and acting on its own, bring about the results which it desires, then the United Nations is regarded as a nuisance, an interfering busybody, which ought to be kept out altogether. We need not take very seriously such a superficial and prejudiced outlook. But we should recognize the need, all the same, for far greater clarity about the nature and functions of the United Nations.

Let me begin by drawing a distinction between the Charter on the one hand, and the functioning of the various organizations on the other. Both of these concepts are implicit in the phrase "United Nations," but they are frequently muddled up. And yet it is vital to distinguish between them.

As far as the Charter is concerned, it is principally a code of conduct which each member nation is expected to observe in its relations with others. I do not need to describe in detail the obligations imposed by it. Those who accept it undertake to follow certain principles, to settle their disputes peacefully, to adopt certain procedures. But on the most important obligation of all, relating to the use of force, I must spend a little more time.

The use of force is by no means ruled out altogether. Article 51 declares that "nothing in the Charter shall impair the inherent right of individual or collective self-defense" if an armed attack occurs against a member of the United Nations; but the state defending itself must report the circumstances immediately to the Security Council and must, if called upon by the Council, desist from using force. At least this is how I interpret the article. Force is also permissible under the Charter — indeed one might say it is obligatory if the Security Council positively enjoins it — when military sanctions, to use an old phrase, are decided on by the Council. A country asked to apply them should then obey the Council and do so. Finally, force may be said to be permissible if the Assembly, by a two-thirds majority or more, recommends the use of it.

Let me pause for a moment and underline the significance of Article 51. *A nation may defend itself or help to defend another nation to which it is allied if there has been an armed attack.* This is the crucial phrase. It is a definition of aggression. Once such aggression has occurred, war against the aggressor is legitimate by the nation attacked and by its allies: it may continue unless and until the Security Council unanimously decides otherwise.

Those who agreed on the Charter evidently decided, in my view rightly, that they must be very precise about when force could be used: the key words are "the right of self-defense if armed attack occurs." *This is the only situation in which, under the Charter, a nation may use force by its own decision.*

Indeed, in Article 2 it is specifically provided that members shall refrain in their international relations from the threat or use of force against the territorial integrity or political independence of any state.

It follows that any idea of force "as a last resort" is beside the point. Unless it is in self-defense or collective defense against armed attack, it is contrary to the charter to use force *even as a last resort*. But, on the other hand, the charter is not "pacifist," as some commentators are inclined to suggest.

I would add, though here I am on slightly more debatable ground, that there is an implied obligation upon those who are prepared to observe this code that they should accept the "decisions" of the United Nations. But great care is needed in interpreting this phrase. When I say "decisions" I mean, first, decisions of the Security Council taken unanimously. Some might say that even when they are not taken unanimously, but taken unanimously except for the veto of the country concerned, an almost equally strong moral obligation applies. I mean, secondly, by decisions of the United Nations, even recommendations of the Assembly, *provided these are taken by really large majorities.* The qualification is vital. A simple majority clearly would not carry with it the same authority, because, owing to the voting system — one state, one vote — it might not be in any way a true reflection of world opinion. But when there are overwhelming majorities, as over Suez, then this is a clear reflection of world opinion, which I believe a nation honestly desiring to follow the principles of the charter ought to accept.

The essence of this obligation to accept decisions is only another way of saying that it is part of the international order which the charter seeks to create that nations do not decide for themselves questions in which their own interest is involved, and that when there is a really clear decision by the United Nations on such questions, then the nations concerned must accept it, even though they disagree with it. But equally — and I must underline the point again — the very nature of both the Security Council and the Assembly makes it inevitable that the United Nations may on many occasions be unable to give this clear decision.

The events of the last few weeks have brought to the surface a number of criticisms about the rules of the Charter in relation to the use of force. Is the phrase "armed attack" sufficiently clear? Would, for example, border raids justify the use of force in self-defense? And if so, on what scale? To this, I think the only answer is that nobody has suggested a clearer definition and that disputes about particular cases have to be handled by the Security Council or the Assembly.

But there are three other criticisms of the Charter of a more fundamental character. First, the definition of aggression in Article 51 rules out the possibility of preventive war. But is preventive war always wrong? We are all familiar with the argument of Israel that Egypt and the other Arab states were preparing war against her, war which might have meant her early elimination, and that the action she took on October 29 was simply designed to prevent this. Here was a case of preventive war which from a common sense angle might seem justified. But it is clearly contrary to the Charter.

The second complaint is that the Charter makes no provision for safeguarding the rights of those countries which suffer a civil wrong. A state may do harm to another state without actually sending an armed force across the frontier. The act may be very damaging. Is the country which suffers the damage to have no protection, and at the same time is it not to be allowed to use force to put the matter right?

The third complaint, which links up with this second one, is that the Charter does not provide for peaceful change. The whole implication of Article 51 is that the *status quo* is to remain. But is a country never justified in using force to bring about a change in the *status quo?*

These criticisms cannot just be pushed aside. A little later, I will try and suggest some answers. But meanwhile it would be wrong to conclude that, because the Charter does not permit a country to use force to deal with these situations, the United Nations can do nothing to put things right, or, again, that the country which believes it is wronged has no alternatives. And I would particularly warn against the idea that, because of these criticisms and the disadvantages which are implied for those who observe the Charter, we ought either to change the definition of aggression in Article 51 or do away with the Charter altogether. The Charter was drafted after a great deal of thought and argument, and, although its wording may not be ideal, it is clearer than any alternative. And clarity in this matter is enormously important.

For the moment then, let us leave the Charter, looked on as a code of conduct, and consider the working of the institutions and, above all, the provision for collective security — that is, for collective action by and through the United Nations against aggression.

Originally, of course, the Security Council was the executive body responsible for dealing with this, and, indeed, with most other problems which reached the United Nations. If one nation attacked another, the Security Council had to consider the matter. But the Security Council is subject to the veto rule in respect of the permanent members, that is, the so-called great powers. Thus the Council can only operate as an instrument of collective security if the great powers are unanimous, or very nearly so. Now this was no accidental decision, but a matter on which both Russia and America insisted. Neither of them was prepared to accept majority decisions in the Security Council on issues of such enormous importance.

Are we, then, to conclude that the Security Council is always going to be useless, because of the veto, as an instrument for insuring collective action against aggression? This would be too pessimistic. The Council could be unanimous in handling minor wars, in which either the great powers were not particularly concerned or where, at any rate, there was no clash between them. As you know, I am one of those who believe that, had it not been for the use of the veto by Britain and France, collective action could have been taken by and through the United Nations on October 30 to stop the war in the Middle East.

Incidentally, it is a mistake to treat the Korean War as an illustration of this kind. The Security Council was unanimous in the case of Korea only because of the accident that Russia had withdrawn from the Council a little while before. The Korean War should really be classified as an instance where Article 51 applied. South Korea was entitled to take action in self-defense under that article. And the United States was entitled to take action under the heading "collective defense."

As for the Assembly, in the charter as originally drafted, it had little effective power for acting against aggression. But since the "uniting for peace" resolution of 1950, a big change has come about. It is now quite likely that in future the Assembly will be the institution to deal with, at any rate, major aggression, rather than the Security Council.

Nevertheless, we must beware of assuming even here that corrective action by the Assembly against aggression is at all easy. There has to be a two-thirds majority. There is, obviously, no assurance that this majority will be forthcoming. It has often been pointed out that a combination of the communist bloc and the Afro-Asian bloc is sufficient to prevent it. But even supposing a two-thirds majority is obtained, it does not follow that effective action will be taken. If a major clash between the great powers is involved, if, in particular, action against a great power is involved, there are likely to be hesitations and anxieties in view of the risk of major war. Such doubts will be overcome only if the other great powers decide that this is a situation which requires that such risks have to be taken. And this in turn is most probable where a collective defense agreement exists which would *in any event*, and without any two-thirds majority vote in the Assembly, have involved resistance to aggression. In that case a resolution of the Assembly carried by the necessary two-thirds majority could, however, lend the weight of public opinion to the cause of collective defense and also perhaps induce other countries to play their part in the defensive action itself.

Apart from this, the use of force on the authority of the Assembly is only likely where the major powers are not themselves seriously engaged. They are not always so engaged. Even if there is a conflict of interest, they may desire to localize a war or even to stop the fighting. And it is possible that this desire may not have shown itself sufficiently clearly at the stage when the Security Council was dealing with the dispute. The Assembly may then provide a second chance in which the public opinion of the world can be brought to bear, both upon the great powers and upon the immediate parties to the dispute, as a result of which the great powers throw their influence behind the Charter and in favor of a peaceful solution.

It is natural enough, in view of these limitations, that the question of how to reform the United Nations should have been discussed so frequently, particularly in recent months. Most of the proposals put forward involve an attempt to establish a greater authority for the United Nations and make it more like a world government. A world government cannot function unless it can take decisions and enforce them. So it is not surprising that one of these proposals is to end the veto in the Security Council. The most obvious difficulty in the way of this is that neither Russia nor, I believe, America would accept it. Since the charter itself provides that it can only be amended if the present members of the Security Council are unanimous, the constitutional obstacle seems insurmountable.

But apart from this, would the change really help? Without doubt, the immediate legal impediment to action by the Security Council would be removed. But what then follows? Is it to be supposed that on a majority vote, even if the majority is quite substantial, there would be an automatic, binding decision to defend the victim of aggression by force?

Once again, if there is an underlying conflict between the great powers on this matter the mere legal right of the Security Council to take action is not the really important thing. The dominant question, *with or without the veto,* is whether the major powers concerned feel that this is an issue on which they must stand firm. They will almost certainly be entitled, even with the veto, to go to the help of the victim of aggression under the collective defense wording of Article 51. *But the real question is whether or not they are prepared to risk a major war.*

I would not deny that, in the absence of the veto, there might be borderline cases where the states concerned felt that the majority decision in their favor helped them to justify intervention, and where such intervention could be swifter, at any rate, by a day or two than it would be after using the "uniting for peace" procedure and relying on a two-thirds majority vote in the Assembly. Furthermore, when the Security Council is handling problems which are less critical and dangerous, the absence of the veto would no doubt lend authority to its majority decisions and make it possible for the Council to go on trying to find peaceful solutions.

There are, however, two other implications of the removal of the veto. First, as soon as the veto disappears, then of course membership of the Security Council becomes extremely important, and it is hardly conceivable that the present system of election could survive. Secondly, it would be wrong to assume that the voting would be the same whether or not the veto applied. If countries know or believe that a particular resolution is going to be vetoed, some of them may be disposed to vote for it, in the certain knowledge that they will never be called upon to take action under it. They might not vote the same way without the protection of the veto. In any event, however, as I have said earlier, the "uniting for peace" procedure has reduced the importance of the Security Council. It was intended to get around the veto, and recent experience shows that this is just what it has done. This brings us, then, to the problem of giving the Assembly, which can and does reach decisions or make recommendations, some kind of force with which to ensure that these decisions are carried out.

Let me say at once that I regard the formation and collection of the international force now employed in Egypt as a very remarkable achievement. It is the first of its kind, and its presence in Egypt has already been of much value both as an excuse for the withdrawal of the Anglo-French forces and as providing a genuine buffer between the Israeli and the Egyptian troops. There is also at least a prospect that this force may patrol the borders of Israel and Egypt, possibly even the borders of the other Arab states, and in that manner make a really valuable contribution to the peace of the Middle East. There may also be other international disputes in which such a force could perform a similar role. Having said this, however, I must draw attention to certain limitations on the kind of force which has just been formed. It is necessary to do so because some people are drawing all sorts of optimistic conclusions which the facts themselves do not justify.

First, then, this force was not expected or intended by the nations who helpfully and loyally contributed to it as a force which was to go to war. It is in this respect totally different from the armies of the United Nations which fought in Korea under the leadership of the United States. It is doubtful if the nations concerned, particularly the Scandinavian states, would have been prepared to lend their troops for such an enterprise if they thought it involved full-scale war with either Egypt or Israel.

Secondly, the force is very limited as regards both manpower and weapons. It could not be a match for even quite a small national army trained in the use of modern weapons. Thirdly, it is strictly temporary and, for the moment, operating only with the consent of the countries in the area concerned. It could not therefore apply a tough decision of the Security Council or the Assembly against a clearly convicted aggressor.

But is it not possible to create a more adequate force? This might take the form either of a firm guarantee from various countries that they would make available troops, weapons, aircraft, and so on in certain quantities when called upon to do so, as contemplated in the Charter, or of a United Nations force recruited directly on the lines of the French Foreign Legion. Whichever course be followed — and undoubtedly the latter is in many respects the more attractive — we are brought up against the old problem of exactly how the decision would be taken to use such a force and under whose control it would operate. I leave on one side here the rather different question of whether such a force would be possible as a consequence of a genuine all-around controlled world disarmament; for the fact is that, if we reach that stage, so many problems of relationships between the great powers will have been solved that the situation will be transformed. In the absence, however, of such all-round disarmament the problem is a very real one.

This is the dilemma. Either the force is a weak one,

an instrument of moral authority alone, in which case it can do what is now being done in Egypt, but not much more. Or the force is a powerful one, equipped with modern weapons, perhaps even with tactical atomic weapons, but in this case the question of exactly when it is to be used and who controls it is an enormously vital one, which has not so far been seriously examined.

It seems unlikely at present that any of the major powers would be prepared to back the establishment of such a force if it were to be controlled by the Assembly on the basis of its present voting system. For even if two-thirds majority decisions were needed to put it into action, would this be acceptable when that majority is based on the one-state, one-vote principle? When in theory there could be a two-thirds majority of the Assembly representing only a small fraction of the world's population?

This brings us to the major problem of the system of voting in the Assembly. It certainly cannot be avoided in any discussion of an effective international force, but it is an issue which really has to be faced as soon as one probes very far into the basis for the Assembly's authority on other matters.

Is it possible to introduce a new basis of voting? Is it possible, for example, to say that the number of votes to which a country is entitled depends on its population? Can we follow the normal democratic principle of one-man, one-vote? I see little chance of this being accepted at present. It would mean that India would have seven or eight times the voting power of Great Britain and twice the voting power of the United States; that Communist China, if and when she is admitted, would have three times the voting power of the United States. It is unlikely that the more wealthy and powerful nations would be prepared to give up so much of their power.

It is true that in the international monetary fund voting depends upon the subscription, and the subscription is determined, roughly speaking, by wealth; but the international monetary fund is a technical agency, and in any event its effectiveness is so dependent upon the support of the wealthy countries that the rule is for the most part accepted. More significant is the fact that in NATO, where you have a group of like-minded allies, it has never proved possible to dispense with the veto, and that in the case of the British Commonwealth no decisions at all are taken on the basis of votes. If this conclusion is accepted, however, and the present system of voting in the Assembly is here to stay, then we must also accept that the authority of the Assembly, except when there are very big majorities, including most larger nations and great powers, is inevitably restricted.

There is, therefore, no denying that, as constituted at present, the United Nations suffers from important limitations. It cannot automatically redress civil wrongs. That was the grievance of Britain and France and other canal users when Colonel Nasser nationalized the canal. It cannot always protect the victim of aggression. It was unable to do so very recently in the case of Hungary. It cannot both pass and enforce judgment in every dispute. It has notably failed to do so in the case of Kashmir.

Nor does it seem likely that these weaknesses will easily be remedied. There is at present little prospect of developing the United Nations into something like world government. It is foolish to blame the United Nations for this. It is simply that the relations between the different countries of the world are still of such a character as to make advance in this direction extremely difficult.

I have not hesitated to draw attention to these limitations because I am convinced that one of the dangers in the present situation is the existence of illusions and misunderstandings on the subject. If public opinion in the democratic countries is led to expect that the United Nations can do things which it subsequently fails to do, there may be a sharp reaction against the whole idea of a system of international law and order. Moreover, we must especially combat the notion that the United Nations is in some way a thing apart and different from the nations which compose it, on which everyone is able to rely. This fallacy is associated with the idea that it is like an ordinary government. It is a dangerous fallacy, because it obscures the need for active leadership. Countries may then speak of "basing their policy on the United Nations," as though all they had to do was to await passively the decisions of some high authority. But clearly if all countries think like this and leave the initiative to others, the United Nations cannot function at all. No! It is the duty of all members to play an active part. But it is the special responsibility of the great powers who believe in the charter to give the necessary leadership.

With this point established, let me now set out the reasons why I believe that, with all its weaknesses, the United Nations can play an important part in meeting the challenge of coexistence.

1. I believe first and foremost that a code of conduct between nations is itself important, especially insofar as it lays down when force may or may not be used. In time, the existence of this code does affect public opinion, and public opinion in its turn has an influence upon the behavior of governments. One has only to consider the change in the public attitude in Great Britain and, I would think, in America also, during these past fifty years.

Despite the outburst of nationalistic feeling during recent weeks, there is no denying the deep sentiments which exist in Britain against the use of force except in self-defense. This has grown up gradually over the years. Such sentiments, however, would not mean much unless there were a reasonably precise definition of aggression by which they could be guided. To blur this definition would be most dangerous, not only in its practical consequences — because it would then be possible to justify the use of force under the Charter far more easily — but also because of the confusion which would thus be created in the public mind. It is important, therefore, to preserve the conception of good behavior by nations and of an international order of some kind, even though it may be an imperfect one.

The importance of these ideas may be measured by the fact that fundamentally both NATO and the British Commonwealth are based upon them. NATO is not just an alliance of friends who undertake to support each other whatever they may do. It specifically accepts the purposes of the United Nations Charter as its own aims. The actual words of Article 1 of the Charter are used in the treaty. NATO will not hold together unless its members abide by these aims. As for the Commonwealth, the fact that at a point during the recent crisis it was described by one of its leading statesmen as "on the verge of dissolution" is sufficient comment. For, insofar as this was true, it was not so much from a clash of interests between the members as because the mother country, in the eyes of some of the members, had acted contrary to the Charter of the United Nations.

2. The United Nations Assembly can at least express world opinion, provided, as I have already ex-

plained, this is clearly shown by very large majorities. Without such an Assembly to show in appropriate cases, by majorities of this character, what different countries think, the picture would be much more confused. The resolutions of the Assembly therefore have an impact. They have an impact most obviously in democracies, where the people are allowed to know what is happening abroad and what other countries think of them, and where it is not regarded as high treason to declare that one's government is wrong. But even for dictatorships the importance of world opinion should not be underestimated. The Soviet government itself is not entirely insensitive on this point. It cannot ignore its own reputation in the uncommitted areas, and if, as in the case of Hungary, it is denounced by the Assembly, then its power and influence, whether directly or through the communist parties, suffers a setback.

3. While the existence of "blocs" is quite inevitable in a world assembly, as it is in any assembly, this is not a fatal weakness. Of course it would be very much better if every delegate were guided in deciding how to vote solely by impartial, objective considerations. And of course this is very far from being the case. But this weakness would only be fatal if the Assembly were completely divided into two groups and there were no "floating vote." But this is not so. There is a "floating vote" in the United Nations Assembly, between the communist countries

on the one side and — say — NATO on the other side. It is no accident that the countries which are, as we say, uncommitted and which constitute this floating vote are themselves among the keenest supporters of the United Nations. But note in passing an important feature of this situation. These countries are mostly ex-colonial countries. They are, therefore, particularly sensitive on what we call colonial issues. This is a matter of which the United States has recently become very conscious — in my view, rightly. It is likely to play an increasingly large part in world affairs and must, therefore, receive further treatment later in these lectures.

4. Even if the notion of a world authority is still very remote, it may be that the much less ambitious conception of a concert of powers — of the great powers of the world being prepared to sit round the table and seek compromise solutions for all the disputes and difficulties that arise — will emerge again. This is what was originally hoped for in 1945. Whether it does emerge will depend principally upon Soviet policy, and possibly on Communist China as well. If it does emerge, then the United Nations is at least a convenient framework, which brings the medium and smaller powers into the picture as well.

It is well known that Stalin, at various times — and his successors have done the same — suggested a kind of carving up of the world between the great powers, particularly between America and Russia, and that the United States has always, very rightly, rejected this. On the other hand, if we are to have any kind of international stability, it is clear that the great powers must somehow or other work together. If they try to do this on their own secretly, there will almost certainly be trouble with the rest of the world. If they do it in the United Nations through the authority of the Security Council, the problem is more soluble.

5. Even if this is optimistic, and the great clash between the communist bloc and the noncommunist world continues with at least its present intensity, it is just as well to have some institution where the countries of both blocs can come together, can get used to talking to and seeing each other, and perhaps from that begin to understand each other. Such an institution does make it possible for any change in policy on the Soviet side to be followed up quickly. One can say in relation to both these last points that it is highly desirable that nations should be obliged to confront each other not in secret (though private talks are sometimes appropriate), but with other nations present, and where they are exposed to the pressures of world opinion. These pressures can and do produce some results. It is difficult to prove beyond a doubt the value of this, or that a particular settlement could not have been reached without the intervention of the United

Nations. Yet one can say that it did exercise an influence on several occasions in the last decade — in the ending of the Berlin Blockade, the granting of independence to Syria and Lebanon, and the settlement of the Indonesian question, to mention only a few instances.

6. We should not neglect or overlook the nonpolitical agencies. I have not time to speak about them here, but quite apart from the value of their work in itself, the fact that they involve joint action in, for instance, the economic sphere is itself likely to have political advantages. For one thing, this avoids introducing power relationships into such questions as technical or economic aid. A technical agency may also acquire a sufficiently good reputation to pave the way for political intervention, for example, in the Middle East.

7. Finally, the United Nations can sometimes provide a piece of machinery, an international device for settling difficult issues, which simply by reason of the fact that it is inherent in and belongs to the United Nations has special advantages. This is obviously true of the international force which has recently been formed for the Middle East; it is also true of the observers under General Burns, even if they were not really adequate to deal with the Arab-Israel border problem. It is true of the commissions and commissioners who have been appointed for various jobs. It is true of the relief organizations

operating in various parts of the world. And it may be that in the future the United Nations will be asked for a time to administer directly certain disputed territories. The conditions for this are not often present. And in a sense the whole notion may be at variance with the idea of independence and self-government which we generally accept. Yet I cannot but feel that if some experiments of this kind could be successfully carried out they might be of great value. The proposal which comes to one's mind at the moment is of course that of the United Nations Organization taking over the Gaza Strip and perhaps a corridor running from there to the Gulf of Aqaba.

It remains for me to say something about the other weaknesses of the Charter, to which I referred earlier: the failure to deal with civil wrongs, to provide for peaceful change, to allow the country threatened with swift extermination to take any preventive action. In theory these drawbacks seem very serious, but I doubt if in practice we need regard them as fatal. For in practice the wronged party is generally able to bring other pressures to bear, short of war, which eventually mitigate the wrong, even if they do not wholly put it right. For instance, Great Britain might well have claimed that she suffered a civil wrong from Persia when the Anglo-Iranian Oil Company agreement was torn up. She did not resort to force, and after three years of stalemate an agreement by no means unsatisfactory to Great Britain was reached.

In the case of the Suez Canal, if there had been a little more patience I believe that an agreement could have been reached with Egypt which would have given the canal users what they wanted without infringing upon the sovereignty of Egypt — an agreement, in short, on the lines of the six principles laid down by the Security Council. This would have been done without the use of force. It is significant that the vast majority of the canal users took this view.

The greatest difficulties emerge when a small country is subject to threats or has suffered civil wrongs from larger countries. Here, all one can say is that a very great responsibility then rests upon the great powers. The case of Israel comes to mind at once. If, in the face of Arab threats, the Tripartite Declaration Powers had both allowed Israel to purchase the arms she wanted earlier, and, while warning her against attacking on her own, given really convincing proofs of their intention to go to her aid if she were attacked, it is unlikely that the recent war in the Middle East would ever have taken place. In this sense, it was undoubtedly as much a failure of France, Britain, and America as anything else.

I am in no way attempting to belittle the importance of these disputes which the United Nations has not been able to settle. But I am claiming that in practice most of them can be dealt with eventually without resort to war. The results may not constitute ideal justice, but they may also be better than any achieved through force — quite apart from the dangers and horrors of resort to war. I must, however, underline the need for the more powerful nations to take the lead in such cases in order to bring about just settlements. Sometimes it may be best to give the lead through the United Nations, by proposing and supporting action by them. If world opinion is strong and nearly unanimous, conditions for this will be favorable. Sometimes it may be more convenient to try to settle a dispute directly. Sometimes the problem is one of mediation; sometimes it is necessary to develop strong pressures which fall short of war. There is no point in attempting to generalize.

I have earlier expressed doubts regarding some of the proposed reforms of the United Nations. But I must put in a plea for one change — in the constitution of the Security Council. The Council is at present based on the situation existing after the end of the Second World War. But since then a great deal has happened. Quite apart from the change in the government of China, there is the rise, to which I have already referred, of the uncommitted areas — in particular, the increasing influence and importance of India — and also the recovery of the defeated countries, Germany and Japan. If we wish the

Security Council to reflect reality, its membership will some day have to be altered.

Both parties in Britain have long taken the view that the continued presence of Nationalist China in the Security Council was an absurdity and that there was no logical reason for refusing to allow Communist China to take her place. Some of you may argue that this concession should not be made without attempting to secure some substantial settlement in exchange. I am not myself convinced of this, because I do not look on membership as a reward for good behavior. I believe the Chinese Communist government should be allowed to take its place because it is the government of China and because I think there is more chance of the United Nations' functioning effectively when it does. True, it would give the communist bloc one more vote in the Assembly, and it would mean that two instead of one votes would be used on occasion to prevent unanimity in the Security Council. These arguments seem to me outweighed by those on the other side.

This, however, is not the only change which should be made. I have already referred to the position of India. When the charter was drawn up India was still a British dominion, without independence. Now she is in a very different position; she could on grounds of population alone stake a most powerful claim for being a permanent member of the Security Council. It might therefore be possible to accept Communist China and to make India a permanent member of the Council at the same time.

There is also the question of the defeated countries. Both Germany and Japan have claims to permanent membership, Japan already, and Germany when reunification has taken place if not before.

But although I would regard a reform of the Security Council on these lines as desirable, let no one imagine that a change of machinery is the most vital one for the future of the United Nations. This will depend ultimately on the wisdom, patience, honesty, and skill of the leading democratic powers. If they are prepared to give full support in their own conduct to the Charter, to give wise and courageous leadership in the Security Council and the Assembly — recognizing both the limitations and the possibilities of the organization — striving where possible to improve its prestige and effectiveness, then the United Nations will, I am convinced, play an increasingly important and valuable role in world affairs. It needs for the moment, and probably will need for a long time, to be supplemented by other international institutions to provide for collective defense against possible aggression under Article 51. NATO is the outstanding example of such an institution. I shall begin my next lecture by examining how it has fared and what part it also has to play in meeting the challenge of coexistence.

II

Coexistence in Europe

IT follows from the argument of my first lecture that the character of the United Nations almost encourages collective defense pacts between countries which feel themselves to be threatened, since there is no clear guarantee that the United Nations itself will provide the necessary security. This is particularly the case if there is serious conflict between the great powers and a real danger of aggression. Some distinguished statesmen — notably Pandit Nehru — have criticized defense pacts on the ground that they divide the world into blocs and lead to countermeasures on the other side. This seems to me to confuse cause and effect. It was only because of the threat of aggression from an already existing communist bloc that the democracies decided to organize collective defense.

Moreover, the need for such pacts arises partly from the existence of a number of relatively small democratic countries which, unlike the satellite communist states, have retained their independence. NATO is both more of a necessity and more of a reality than the Warsaw Pact, which only formalizes an already existing situation.

In effect, what such pacts do is to try to preserve the balance of power. To the more idealistic conception of how peace should be preserved, as enshrined in the charter, there has to be attached as a kind of supplement the realistic method often adopted in the past. For my part I have never looked on the balance of power as an evil thing which is itself the cause of war. The balance of power is simply an attempt to ensure that no one power or group of powers occupies such a dominating position that the temptation to indulge in aggressive war against others is overwhelming. If the balance is there, runs the doctrine, then it will provide a deterrent against attack.

No one will deny that in these postwar years there *has* been serious conflict between the great powers and at times danger of aggression. The complete defeat of Germany meant that Russia was bound to be by far the greatest power in Europe — indeed, that even a combination of the other European powers could not hope to prevail against her. Her advance into Europe at the end of the war was followed by tough cold war tactics and by a series of aggressive moves, designed, while threatening the democracies, to strengthen her own strategic position. The dispute with Persia in 1946, the attempt to secure power in Greece, the successful *coup d'état* in Czechoslovakia, the attempt to starve West Berlin into submission, and, finally, the boycott of Yugoslavia, combined at times with military threats — all these were part of Stalin's policy. The final move was the attack on South Korea in 1950 — the only one which led to definite fighting, and which, perhaps for that reason, had the most decisive influence upon the West.

Moreover, while all these steps were taken, the Soviet Union was adamantly refusing to come to terms on virtually any of the outstanding problems left over at the end of the war, and was also maintaining her armed forces at a level far above that to which the Western powers had reduced theirs.

That Russia, so powerful in Europe and with such obviously aggressive intentions, did not succeed in imposing its will upon the West was surely due to the fact that the United States alone in the early postwar years possessed the atom bomb, and was prepared, if need be, to use it. It is possible that, even apart from this, Russia's ambitions might have been curbed or sated and that she would not have attempted to push farther west, but one can hardly feel any conviction on the point.

Why was it, however, if in the years 1945 to 1949, without NATO, without rearmament, Russia was held at bay by the atom bomb, that this was not thought sufficient in the years which followed? I do not recall that at the time any very clear answer was given to this question — if indeed the question was then clearly put. The answers I shall give now may therefore be partly rationalizations. But I would say, first, that there was always the possibility, which became a certainty, that Russia would herself develop the production of atom and, later, hydrogen bombs. Once she had done this the bombs would balance each other out and there would be a stalemate; the United States would be loath to use these fearful weapons first, lest she be faced with retaliation from Russia. But this led to the danger that Stalin, having, so to speak, canceled out the nuclear weapons, might use conventional forces, in which the Russians had a decided advantage. Thus it became necessary for the Western democracies to develop their own conventional defenses.

Secondly, even if nuclear weapons were going to be used in defense against Soviet attack — and opinion moved later more and more to this assumption — conventional forces were needed to provide time.

The third reason was that, as Soviet pressure increased, the need for Western Europe to be certain of United States backing grew stronger. It was needed to boost their morale and as a counterblast to the most effective of all communist propaganda — the notion that sooner or later Russia would win. We all know the story, which illustrates the defeatism in Western Europe in the late 1940's, of the man who asked his friend what he was going to do in the next war. "Join the resistance movement," was the reply.

NATO was formed in 1949 and it was followed after the Korean War by the adoption of rearmament programs both in the United States and in Western Europe; and, at the end of 1950, when the situation in Europe appeared to be most dangerous, by the commitment on the part of the United States to maintain forces in Europe, on the condition that the Allied forces must include substantial German contingents — which in turn meant the rearmament of Germany.

In view of criticisms which I shall shortly develop, let me place on record certain facts about NATO. First, it was and still is a *real* alliance. Since history is strewn with the wreckages of unreal alliances, it is as well to emphasize this. It is not a paper pact. Nobody doubts that under certain conditions it would operate. It has a military headquarters of its own and an Allied Command in existence today.

Secondly, the presence of United States troops in Europe is also a reality: since this is the first occasion that such a commitment has been accepted in peacetime by America, it has special significance. Thirdly, the members of NATO are countries which have a great deal in common. They have, most of them, or the most powerful of them, been allies in two world wars. Some of them share a common language. To a large extent they enjoy a common civilization and at least similar political institutions.

Fourthly, NATO is a purely defensive alliance — designed to be effective in relation to clearly defined frontiers. There can be few alliances which have been quite so specific.

Fifthly, in a limited field it has been highly successful. A very large number of airfields have been built and an elaborate radar structure to detect the proximity of enemy aircraft.

Finally, as a result of these various things, *NATO has made resistance to aggression certain.* It is doubtful if without it the Russians would have been convinced of immediate American intervention — intervention *in time* to prevent victory for the aggressors.

The building up of NATO has also been accompanied by a considerable strengthening of other ties between America and Europe, within Europe itself, and between Britain and Europe. There are the O.E.E.C., the Council of Europe, the Coal and Steel Community, and now the Euratom project. Moreover, partly arising out of O.E.E.C., there is now the suggestion of a common market for some countries and a free trade area for many more.

The European movement may not have made as much headway as its supporters desired, but it has certainly achieved some change in outlook. The European people today feel closer to one another than ever before. This would probably not have happened without the basic Atlantic Alliance — NATO.

Having said all that, however, I must now draw attention to a number of weaknesses in this key organization.

First, on the purely military plane. Although the rearmament plans of the West involved substantial increases in conventional forces, it was never the intention that they would be able to match Russian manpower precisely. The rearmament programs in the West did not aim so high. A smaller force, it was decided, would be sufficient for a purely deterrent purpose. The idea was to have enough ground troops to make it impossible for the Russians to win a surprise blitzkrieg — enough troops to resist at least for a sufficient time before the heavier weapons — first the atom, and then the hydrogen, bomb — could be brought into use. With this end in view, it was decided in 1952 that the West should aim at some 85 divisions.

As a cold fact, the West has never been in sight of this target.

It is true that the target itself was not maintained for very long. Development of *tactical* nuclear weapons reduced the need for man power; and, although these weapons are scarcely available today, the NATO Command appears to have reduced its requirements from 85 divisions to 30, of which 12 are to be provided by Germany. If there is a clear target today, this is it.

We appear, however, to be almost as far from this target as from the earlier one. France has removed most of the troops which she should have had in Europe to North Africa, where she is employing an army of some 400,000 men to protect the French settlers and put down the Arab rebellion. Germany has been very slow in providing her contingents and has herself, on her own initiative, reduced her manpower figure from 500,000 to 300,000 men. At the same time, the United Kingdom and the United States, who have provided the contingents required from them — four and five divisions — are now speaking of reducing them. In the light of all this, it seems improbable that General Norstad could muster today much more than half the 30 divisions regarded by his predecessor as necessary.

I must emphasize again that the 30 divisions, and therefore, presumably, still more the 15 divisions or whatever is available, are supposed to be provided with nuclear tactical weapons. But in this nuclear field, the position can only be described as decidedly confused.

First, so far as the ultimate weapon is concerned — the deterrent, the hydrogen bomb — only the

United States at present possesses this. It is entirely in its hands as to whether the bomb should or should not be used. It would be a fearful decision to take in the face of an attack with conventional forces, however powerful, because of the horrific effects of the bomb and the virtual certainty of retaliation not only on Europe but on America also. It would be understandable if the United States hesitated, even though this meant the defeat of land forces in Europe. At any rate, Western Europe could not be sure. Precisely because the decision on this remains a matter for the United States, precisely because there are inevitable doubts as to when and whether the decision to threaten to use the bomb would be taken, the United Kingdom has felt obliged at vast expenditure to manufacture the hydrogen bomb herself. It may be that there was no alternative, that the idea of any common control over the use of this fearful weapon was utopian; but if so a very great additional strain was placed upon the resources of the Western democracies.

Quite apart from difficulties over the hydrogen bomb, it is not absolutely certain that tactical nuclear weapons will really be available. Recently, the United States Congress has agreed that the forces of NATO shall receive the weapons themselves from the United States, but not the actual warheads. These, presumably, are to remain under the control of the American army.

Once again, therefore, doubts arise about how far the Allied forces are going to be properly equipped. Once again, this would not matter if when the time came there was certainty about the decision of the United States. But can there be such certainty? Although it may seem probable that the President or Congress would be more likely to give permission for the warheads to be fitted to the atomic shells than for the actual use of the hydrogen bomb, some will argue, nevertheless, that the use of nuclear tactical weapons will only be the first step down a slippery slope which will end with the H-bomb. Those who argue thus might exercise sufficient influence to paralyze the whole of the Western force. If the Russians think that this is likely to happen, then the deterrent effect of NATO will have become negligible.

I can give a ready illustration of the point. When the Russian tanks recently moved into Hungary, there was a short period during which Austria appeared to be threatened. There were stories of several armored divisions moving to the Austrian frontier. Supposing that, in fact, the Russians had decided to pick a quarrel with Austria over, say, the escape of refugees, and had advanced across the border. What would the West have done? Would the United States have been prepared to threaten the use of the H-bomb or even of tactical atomic weapons? If not, what conventional forces could have been made available?

There is another problem ahead. There is no doubt whatever that within the next few years there will be developed what is known as the intercontinental ballistic missile — rockets, fitted with nuclear warheads, to travel thousands of miles at fantastic speeds. When such weapons have been manufactured, a new military tactical situation will emerge.

At present, the United States has a direct military need for Western Europe, because some of the bases from which bombers can take off with the H-bombs are located there. Although recent developments have made possible direct flights from the United States to Russia and back, yet bases in Europe are also required, in the event of Soviet aggression, to bring to bear on Russia the greatest possible variety in counterattack. It is thought desirable in this event to have as many different bombers as possible attacking from different directions.

Suppose, however, that the bases are no longer necessary because of the development of the intercontinental ballistic missile? What, then, will be the attitude of the United States to Europe? Will she still desire the alliance as before? Will it still matter to her whether Europe remains free or is dominated by communism? I have little doubt about the answer. I have always held that United States policy was not determined so much as some people think by self-interest alone. I believe that the sentimental ties between Western Europe and the United States are so powerful that no American government would really sacrifice Europe to such a fate.

But since the intercontinental ballistic missile is only a more effective carrier for a nuclear or thermo-nuclear bomb, exactly the same queries arise about the threat to use it as with the hydrogen bomb. If the United States is the only NATO power to possess this weapon, how can the other members be sure it will be used in defense of Europe? Inevitable though they may be, these uncertainties about the use of nuclear weapons have a decidedly unsettling effect upon NATO and its members.

The plain fact, then, is that all that exists in the way of Western defenses in Europe today is a trip wire, with no absolute certainty of exactly what the trip wire would set off. One can hardly describe that as a very impressive achievement, particularly in view of the remarkably fine qualities of the military commanders at SHAPE.

To be sure, the circumstances have been made extraordinarily difficult by the technical developments and the difficulty of working out sufficiently quickly the full military implications of these. But I fear this is not the whole story.

We have witnessed in recent years in NATO the familiar processes of democracy when the danger of aggression is not so clear. One country after another has sought to proclaim that it was doing more than any of the other Allies in relation to its capabilities. One country after another has proposed to cut down on defense. One country after another has pleaded obligations elsewhere.

It is a characteristic of democracy that people are free to express their preferences. And their preferences are, naturally, for a better time, more leisure, lower taxes, and all the other good things of life. Unless they see an absolute necessity for making sacrifices, they will not be disposed to do so, and a political party which ignores these human inclinations will find it hard to win sufficient votes. That is the background to these last few years. The truth is that, unless a positive effort is made to avoid this kind of thing, it will always happen.

I am not saying that anything very disastrous has in fact occurred. It is possible that other changes have brought greater security. But it would be far better if a reduction in military effort were the result of deliberate policy decisions, collectively taken, rather than a by-product of the slow decline in the unity of the Alliance.

I myself believe that these consequences could have been avoided if at the beginning it had been settled that there should be a common defense plan, and agreement among the member countries on just how it should be fulfilled, both financially and materially. This was what we contemplated in the early days of NATO and of rearmament. It was just such a conception that we were working on at the NATO Conference at Ottawa in 1951. It was never carried out. Partly, no doubt, it was disturbed by the nuclear developments to which I have referred. Partly, it was affected by the change in Russian tactics. Partly, I am afraid, it was due to the break in continuity resulting from governmental changes in different democratic countries and the subsequent failure to maintain the élan of the alliance.

Perhaps, too, behind all this lies something more fundamental. Can we really envisage an effective military defense unless the countries concerned operate what amounts to a common foreign policy? If they do not, the centrifugal tendencies are likely in time to be overwhelming.

This brings me to a second weakness of NATO. The greatest strain upon relations between the NATO countries has arisen not so much from problems within the strict NATO area — Europe — but from problems thrown up outside. It is one of the characteristics of the NATO Alliance that many members of it have non-European interests. And these non-European interests are by no means held in common. Even if, in other parts of the world, America, Britain, and France do desire jointly to resist communist expansion, they sometimes form very different judgments about the way in which such resistance should be conducted.

Let me illustrate this point. The Korean War,

although involving joint action — an allied command, a common front in Korea itself — in fact imposed a severe strain on European Atlantic relations. This was due more than anything else to the difference in the burden carried. For America, the Korean War was very much a real war. The casualties were heavy and affected almost every town in the country. In Britain — and, still more, in other countries in Europe — it was a far-away police action in which very limited forces were involved — a far-away police action of the kind, incidentally, to which European countries, far more than the United States, were accustomed in their history.

I have often thought that the impact would have been very different if Europe had provided more contingents in Korea, and America more contingents in Europe or, indeed, in other parts of the world; but the degree of co-operation between the members of the Alliance was not such as to make this possible.

There were also other irritants. There was the difference of attitude to Communist China reflected in the different rules applied about trading with China, and the difficult question of Formosa and the offshore islands. It was no doubt inevitable that the United States attitude to some of these problems should be different from that of Europe, yet one cannot but feel that too little effort was made to bring about a common understanding.

Another illustration of the impact upon NATO of

developments outside the NATO area is North Africa. Undoubtedly, the campaign there has done much harm to relations between France and America and to some extent France and Britain. There is the sheer military burden imposed upon France and the fact that in consequence she has had to reduce forces in Europe by such a substantial amount. And behind this there is the fear or suspicion in France that the United States really sides with the Arabs. I have even heard a Frenchman say that he believed that the United States was behind the whole revolt because it wished to take over North Africa!

As for the United Kingdom, she too has her outside interests which have damaged good relations in NATO. I need hardly underline this now, in view of recent events. Quite apart from the Middle East, the situation in Cyprus has caused very grave friction in NATO between Turkey and Greece, and also had some impact on relations between Britain and the United States.

The trouble in all these cases is that there has been no common policy and almost no effort to create one. Each of the countries concerned decides for itself in areas outside Europe, and in deciding for itself sometimes finds that it is in conflict with another NATO country.

Moreover, these external problems have a military impact. They have a bearing on what each country feels it can do as a fair share of the arms burden in Europe. Each country wants to run on its own its policy in other parts of the world, but to claim credit or help for this when it comes to deciding its obligations to NATO.

The third weakness of NATO is in European policy itself. It is associated with the problem of Germany. Just as America in Korea, France in North Africa, and Britain in the Middle East have interests which are thought to be not identical with the interests of other NATO countries, so Germany has her analogous problem of reunification. Here, too, there has been a deep and fundamental difference of outlook. To Western Germany, reunification is of vital concern. It is a subject upon which most Germans feel very deeply. But this desire for reunification is not shared to the same extent by the peoples of other NATO countries, particularly those who have suffered in the past from German invasion. Some of them feel that perhaps it is as well that Germany should remain weak and divided. On the whole, one can perhaps be thankful that these divergencies have not caused more trouble, and perhaps this itself is something of a tribute to NATO.

Be that as it may, nobody can really say that the German problem is in a satisfactory condition at present. Despite the decisions on rearmament and her membership of NATO, Germany is even now not really fully integrated into the West. She has a

natural reluctance to involve herself in the burden
of rearmament, which to some people may even seem
praiseworthy in view of her past history! She sees
that membership of NATO and the decision to re-
arm have not apparently brought reunification any
nearer, although this was the claim always made by
the German chancellor. She sees that NATO itself is
not so powerful as at one time was expected. She
knows well that the NATO contingents, even with
her own limited forces, will be little more than a trip
wire. She is not convinced that German soil is going
to be defended to the end. She feels, on the contrary,
that, as things are, it is likely to be abandoned in the
early stages of any conflict with Russia. It is hardly
surprising in all these circumstances, and bearing in
mind the intense feeling about reunification, that the
German people from time to time turn to the possibility of a different pattern of relationships, to the
possibility of some agreement which Germany might
make on her own with Russia.

We must conclude, then, that, at any rate in conventional forces and readiness for immediate action,
NATO is still militarily weak, that its members have
been distracted and divided by a series of events in
other parts of the world, and that even in Europe
itself the central political problem of Germany remains unsolved.

Happily, however, if the West has its problems
and troubles, so also has the Soviet Union. We

have to thank the incredible heroism of the Hungarians, and the firm courage of the Poles, for bringing this home to us in the last few months.

Let us not underestimate the enormous significance of what they have done. They have thrown a most vivid light, now apparent to the rest of the world, upon the real feelings of the peoples of the satellite countries; they have set an example to these peoples of resistance to the armed might of Russia which will surely never be forgotten; they have shown that the rule of the communist puppet governments is only kept in being by the tanks and artillery of the Soviet army. They have, by their amazingly prolonged resistance, forced the Russian government to take action which has discredited the communist parties and communist propaganda everywhere else in the world.

Finally, these events have lifted from our hearts and minds a terrible burden of depression which had settled there — the feeling that there was no hope, no chance of effective resistance by a people against a modern totalitarian dictatorship — the feeling indeed that the combination of indoctrination and terror was so powerful that in time it would produce a robot-like race in whom the desire for freedom itself had died. How wrong we were! And how exhilarating to find that in the very section of the community most completely exposed to the communist monopoly of education and propaganda — the younger generation — opposition to the regime and to communist values is strongest!

Why did the revolt take place? Apart from the general background described in my first lecture, it seems clear that the revolutionary movements, both in Poland and in Hungary, really sprang from three sources. First, they were a spontaneous protest against the almost intolerable economic conditions prevailing in both countries. To this extent, they were the result of a very foolish economic policy adopted by the Soviet Union, a policy of extreme exploitation, which may have brought temporary direct benefit to the people of Russia but which produced great strains and stresses in the exploited countries.

Secondly, the revolutions were a protest against political repression. No doubt this is what particularly influenced the intelligentsia, which in both countries, but particularly in Hungary, appears to have played a leading part in the revolution. Thirdly, of course, these movements were strongly nationalist and directed against Russian domination over their countries because it was foreign.

I do not propose to discuss the issue of whether or not we should have intervened with armed force on the side of Hungary. Everybody, I think, knows the answer. Quite apart from the physical difficulties owing to the neutralization of Austria, any attempt to do so would have involved a pretty serious risk of a third world war.

It may be said, "Was not that a risk for Russia as well?" That is true, but the question of whether you are prepared to take a risk of that kind does not only turn on your cool calculation of what the other country is going to do: it also turns on how far your mind is prepared to treat the whole situation as one in which you are prepared to stake everything.

The plain fact is that, in our defense planning and its political framework, we did not envisage such a situation developing out of a rising behind the Iron Curtain. Our flash points were such events as the blockade of Berlin, the threat to Yugoslavia, and always the possibility of Russian troops advancing directly into Western Germany. But for us to take the initiative in breaking through the Iron Curtain to help people on the other side of it was a prospect for which we had never really provided.

Faced with the new situation, what will the Russians do? It seems clear that, so far at any rate, they are determined to try to retain these countries as political satellites. They are probably prepared, in order to achieve this aim, to improve economic conditions and up to a point to introduce more liberal political measures. The question, however, is whether these policies are capable of producing a new stability.

Undoubtedly, economic improvement would make a considerable difference; we should not underestimate its effect. On the other hand, greater political freedom generally leads to demands for still more freedom; and if at the same time the Russians attempt to hold these countries very much under their own control, they will only fan the flames of nationalism further.

I do not pretend to be in the least certain about this. I do not think it likely that the Russians can return to pure Stalinist tactics, partly because there is no Stalin in Russia today and partly because the movement away from this, not only in the satellite states but in Russia itself, has already become too powerful. It is, perhaps, conceivable that a new military dictatorship could be set up, but I doubt if in the satellite countries it would have a sufficient local basis to give it any degree of stability. It is clear that the Russians cannot rely on the armies of these countries against the local inhabitants. It is possible that in the case of Poland, as in Yugoslavia, some form of national communism may survive. But on the whole I think it most likely that the movement of opinion both within the satellite states and Russia will continue to create an unstable and fluid situation. On that assumption, what kind of policy should we try to follow in Europe?

First of all, as regards Germany, it is surely clear

that the present situation cannot be allowed to continue indefinitely. In Germany itself, there is every prospect that after the next election there will be a change of government in some form and that the new government will be expected either to persuade its Western allies to put forward new initiatives or itself to instigate direct talks with Russia on the problem of reunification.

But, secondly, as has recently been pointed out by the German foreign minister, there is the question of what will happen if a rising takes place in East Germany. In 1953, West Germany had no armed forces. But it will soon have some. It will not be easy to prevent their going to the help of their compatriots in East Germany if anything like a Hungarian rising occurs there. Yet if this were to happen, all Europe might be faced with a highly dangerous situation; for it is most unlikely that the Russians would be prepared to stand aside. If they intervened, then exactly what would be the attitude of Germany's allies in NATO?

The aims of the West in this situation are obvious enough. We wish to see the satellite states regain their freedom without war or any serious consequential risk of a future war.

But what of the Russian outlook? It is as well to try and understand this, since a peaceful solution must ultimately depend on the willingness of Russia to make terms with us. There is little doubt that

Russia would be glad to avoid the dangerous position created by a rising in East Germany and that it will try to prevent this by keeping a very tight hand on the Communist Party and the puppet government there. But the Russians may not find it so easy. In general they face a very grave dilemma in their policy toward the satellite states. If they insist on rigid control over the local communist parties, they may create exactly the situations which have already developed in Poland and Hungary. If, on the other hand, they are content to give up their control, then they have no reliable instrument with which to assert themselves except the Soviet army. Therefore, for them as well as for the West a continuation of the present situation is not going to be at all easy.

What change would they be prepared to contemplate, and at what price? The key surely is security. They are probably not so worried about this as they were a few years ago. The development of nuclear weapons must have given them a great deal of confidence about any possible land attack from the West. For we may fairly assume that they will be much less inhibited in the use of such weapons in defense than the West would be.

If then they face the prospect of grave political trouble in the satellite states, if in any event they have to yield up much of the economic advantages they have gained from exploitation in recent years, if the strategic value of these territories has declined, if in addition they could obtain some further concessions on security, is it not just conceivable that the Russians might be willing on their side to withdraw their forces from the satellite states?

It seems to me that the prospect is at least worth exploring. And while governments must no doubt be very cautious in any public pronouncements on such a possibility, if only not to prejudice future negotiations, perhaps I might be allowed to exercise one of the privileges of opposition and pursue the matter further.

The path to be followed seems to me an extension of the Eden Plan put forward in 1955. It was at that time proposed that there should be a withdrawal of forces from the frontier between East and West Germany, leaving within Germany itself a zone in which there were no foreign troops. Would it not be possible to extend the area of such a zone until it covered, say, the whole of Germany, Poland, Czechoslovakia, and Hungary, and, if possible, Romania and Bulgaria?

The withdrawal could be a gradual one, taking place over a period of time. It would have to be subject to control, as would also the size and character of whatever national forces it was agreed that the countries in question should possess. But here the latest proposals of the Russians themselves for a zone in which there would be both aerial and ground controls might be appropriately introduced. Indeed, one could envisage the whole plan as forming part of a wider move toward a comprehensive disarmament agreement between the great powers.

In the early stages it might be advisable to leave the alliances unchanged. To begin with, both NATO and the Warsaw Pact might continue. But if foreign troops withdrew, it is doubtful whether this situation could last long. Indeed, the Russians might refuse to contemplate the plan without neutralization on both sides from the start. They would assume, no doubt, that the satellite countries would prefer to be neutral, and they would therefore wish to ensure that Germany was neutral as well. I believe that this is a risk which we ought to take.

I was myself never favorable to the idea of a neutralized Germany as the condition for reunification alone. I believed that if a reunified Germany were neutralized and outside NATO, there was a real danger that in time the Russians would come to dominate her. One envisaged the Russian tanks suddenly moving across the frontiers, and before long the whole of the territory under Soviet control. And there was the other danger of the communists staging a *coup d'état* internally while the West looked on impotent. I had little faith that the democracies would move quickly enough to prevent this. There was also the different, but equally sinister, possibility — that Russia would make a deal with Germany at the expense of Poland, as had happened in the past.

But none of these dangers would be serious in a plan involving a much wider neutral bloc and the withdrawal of the Red Army to Russia. Moreover, the weakening of the Communist Party in Eastern and Central Europe would greatly reduce any risks of this kind.

Finally, together with the permanent controls on arms in these territories, there should be a multi-lateral European security plan, in which the various states in the neutral zone would have their territories guaranteed by the great powers as well as by each other.

This brings me to one other matter which would have to be cleared up — the settlement of the frontiers of Germany and Poland. It seems most unlikely that any substantial change can be made in the existing frontiers. The populations have moved and settled down, and I do not believe that either the Poles or the Russians would agree to drastic revision. Both Dr. Carlo Schmidt and Mr. Brentano deserve much credit for their courage in facing this issue in recent speeches. I hope that the Germans them-selves would feel that the renunciation of claims to the pre-1945 territories would be a price worth pay-ing for reunification and the freedom of the satellite countries.

Finally, I must underline that in any plan of this kind American troops should stay in Europe — in the Low Countries, in France, and in Britain. In short, NATO should not retreat farther back than the frontiers of Germany.

I should be the first to recognize that any such plan as I have outlined could only be brought about as a result of very long negotiations and subject to a great deal of modification. The first stage would be for the Western powers to try to reach agreement on it themselves. As an outsider, one can only put forward these ideas in very general terms. Indeed, it would be foolish to try to be too specific. But it seems to me, apart from anything else, that we owe it to the peoples of the satellite countries at least to examine what can be done to win freedom for them by diplomatic means.

There is one further subject to which I must pay some attention in this lecture: European unity. Wherever I go in America, I am asked by American friends about the attitude of Britain toward European unity. Recent events have given a new emphasis to this subject.

The United Kingdom is, of course, fully committed militarily to the defense of Western Europe. I do not think that even if there were to be a withdrawal of the United States from Europe, this would affect our position. We are bound by the Paris Agreements of 1954, and I am sure that any British government would uphold them. Secondly, we play, and will continue to play, a large part in intergovernmental organizations such as the O.E.E.C.

Thirdly, there is a strong consensus of opinion in Britain in favor of our joining the proposed free trade area — subject to various safeguards — though not the so-called "common market," which the six inner countries seem likely to establish. Fourthly, we may very well be closely associated with other functional institutions, such as the proposed Euratom.

Finally, there has been a considerable development of cultural and social ties between Britain and Europe since the war; many more British people go to Europe for holidays and there is rather more general sentiment in favor of closer association with the European peoples.

Having said all this, however, I must emphasize the limits to any formal changes. It is most unlikely that any British government will seriously contemplate joining a European political federation. There are deep and profound reasons for this.

The United Kingdom, although part of Europe, is also still the center of the Commonwealth. It does half its trade with Commonwealth countries. The Commonwealth is something in which many of us have pride not because we are "imperialists" but for precisely the opposite reason. We are proud that out of a colonial empire there has been and is being developed an association of free, independent, self-governing states, containing many different races, colors, and religions. We feel, particularly in my party, that it is a valuable bridge between East and West. We should not like to weaken it in any way.

There is also some anxiety lest a closer partici-pation in Europe might mean not only separating us from the Commonwealth but also linking us up positively with a group of countries some of which seem to have rather different views from ours on colonial policy. There is no denying that some of the recent pleas in Britain for closer unity with Europe reflect irritation with what is supposed to be America's lack of sympathy with our Middle East policy and our alleged "colonialism." European gov-ernments, it is held, precisely because they have or have had colonies, appreciate our point of view bet-ter. I must emphasize that this is the outlook of a small section of our community only. Many of us take a very different view and are indeed deeply disturbed at the implications of such ideas.

Secondly, we also feel that we have a special rela-tionship with the United States. We would not wish any closer ties with Europe to weaken our ties with you. Sometimes we are afraid that they might. And, candidly, the only way to give us that assurance is for the closer links with Europe to be forged only within a more closely knit Atlantic community.

We cannot help feeling that the military organizations in which we have participated in Europe without America have been rather unsuccessful. The Brussels Pact, which preceded NATO, has been completely dwarfed by it. The Western European Union, heralded with much enthusiasm at the time of the Paris Agreements, does not appear to have made any headway.

Then there are quite reasonable doubts about what exactly is meant by Europe: where does it begin, and where does it end? If German reunification is to be realized, will the reunified Germany be in any such federation?

Nor are we greatly impressed with the idea, which should make little appeal to the United States, that if we go into Europe we can with the other European countries create a third force to hold the balance between Russia and America. I prefer a comment made about this proposal some years ago that there was too much "third" and too little "force" about it!

There are other reasons for hesitation. Some of the political systems in Western Europe are very different from our own. We are not accustomed to coalition governments; and a system of successive coalitions, each of which lasts for a few months and then gives way to another, makes no appeal to us. It may be a small point, but it is the kind of point which does impress politicians — and it will be the politicians who will make the ultimate decision.

And don't underrate the language problem. We are bad linguists!

I realize that this may seem depressingly negative. But so many of my American friends have illusions about this matter that I thought I had better speak plainly. Do not misunderstand me. We are already more closely associated with Europe. The process will be carried further, I believe, in the economic field. But big political developments seem to me unlikely. For my part, while I should be ready to see us more closely associated with a more intimate continental community, just as we are, for instance, in the steel and coal community, I should be reluctant for us to move any closer to this continental community unless the United States moves along, too — even if, so to speak, it is further away from them than we are. I should prefer to see any closer integration taking place within a more vital and more living Atlantic community.

It is of course possible that opinion in Britain on these matters may change. If the commonwealth were to break up, if Canada were to throw in her lot wholly with the United States, and Australia and New Zealand as well, if the Asian members of the commonwealth were to go their own way — if, in short, we were left with nothing but little England, then no doubt we should have a far greater incentive to join Europe. But do not, please, imagine that there is any desire for this in England now! All these things might conceivably happen to us, but they would be looked on by most people as a misfortune, not a blessing!

And do not be misled by a certain amount of foolish prejudice which is to be observed in some quarters in Britain at the moment. There are people who are talking in terms of a third force because they are angry with America. There are people who are turning to Europe because they feel that they have more sympathetic friends in Europe. But this is not likely to last. The idea will not appeal to any large body of supporters in the United Kingdom. Describe it, if you like, as post-Suez depression. I hope the depression will be over soon.

In the meantime, to go back to where I began this lecture, so long as Russian policy remains fundamentally aggressive, so long as there is no agreed and controlled disarmament, so long as the major problems of the world are unsettled, we cannot afford to renounce NATO.

But is is not enough to say that we stand by it. As I said earlier, there is an inevitable tendency among democracies for alliances to break up unless a positive effort is made to hold them together. We need to make that positive effort. I believe that this is a matter of understanding rather than new machinery. The report of the three "Wise Men" is surely right. What we need is an understanding that no member of NATO will take action on its own, *in any part of the world,* which affects other members of the alliance without consulting them. Consultation, of course, does not mean obligation to agree. But it does mean taking seriously what your friends say. It does mean making an effort to get agreement. I cannot, myself, see any possibility of drawing a distinction on a geographical basis, so that we consult about one area and not about another. Things are too much mixed up for that. The shortage of oil in Europe is grim evidence of it!

I do not think there is really any doubt about the feeling among the members of NATO regarding the Anglo-French action in the Middle East. There is no need to rake over the coals. I hope that what has happened may serve as a warning to all of us, and that, instead of other members of NATO following this example, there will be a revulsion against anybody doing anything of the kind again.

In pleading for this closer unity, I am not saying that we should become tougher either in the military or political field. On the contrary, I believe that, despite any superficial signs to the contrary, recent events do hold out the possibility that a more flexible foreign policy may be very fruitful. But this policy should be worked out by us together. Indeed, it is only on that basis that is likely to succeed. I do not propose to discuss here the mechanical problems of co-operation. The essential point is surely that the representatives who sit in Paris should have the most intimate contact with and the full confidence of their governments.

I profoundly hope that the United States will do all it can to encourage this closer co-operation between the Atlantic countries. I realize that, at the moment, there are voices talking of different policies of a new line involving more distant rather than more intimate relations between America and Europe. But since this new line is bound up with the relations between America and other parts of the world, I must leave any further thoughts about it until we have had a look at those other territories and the policies which might be adopted by the West in its relations with them. This is what I propose to do in my third lecture.

III

The Uncommitted Areas

THE phrase "uncommitted areas" is one which has come into frequent use recently. There is no precise, generally accepted definition, but by it I mean noncommunist states in Asia and Africa not closely linked with the Western powers in military alliances. Inevitably, there are blurred edges. Iraq, Iran, and Pakistan are all borderline cases, although they are members of the Bagdad Pact. On the whole I count them among the uncommitted areas for the purposes of this lecture. Turkey, on the other hand, as a full member of NATO, I would definitely exclude. Japan is another borderline case. For the moment, I am inclined to exclude it on account of its close relationship with the United States, but it certainly could become an uncommitted area, even if it is not so already. On the other hand, I would include most of the remaining colonial territories in Africa and Asia. Even though the governments are committed — being Western powers — the same can hardly be said of the peoples. It seems unlikely that many of them, when they obtain independence, will desire to be closely linked with the Western military alliances.

By far the most important uncommitted nations are India and the Arab countries. Between them, they alone include some 450 million people. When one adds the other uncommitted states, we have a figure of about 600 million people — or a quarter of the world's population.

It would obviously be foolish to treat all these countries as though they were in exactly the same position. They have different problems, different backgrounds, different institutions. Nevertheless, apart from the Near or Middle East, I do not propose to conduct a grand survey nation by nation, or even area by area, giving in respect to each the kind of solution which I think appropriate. There is no time for this, and I have not got the necessary qualifications. Moreover, with the differences go some very striking similarities — similarities which justify a more general treatment.

Nearly all these countries are ex-colonial territories. They were, until recently, governed by other countries. Nearly all are exceedingly poor compared with the West. Nearly all are still in the preindustrial stage, predominantly agricultural in character, exporting chiefly raw materials and food. They contain peoples of a darker color than those in the West. Although racially mixed, they side instinctively with the darker colored peoples in any clash with the whites. Indeed, they have developed in recent years quite a strong sense of solidarity with each other, which sometimes produces hostility toward Western policies which appear to be trying to divide them from one another.

Their numbers alone, particularly in the case of India, make it certain that, as long as they remain independent, these countries are going to be more and more important in world affairs. This process will be hastened both by economic development, which in some form or other will almost certainly take place, and by the spread of egalitarian ideas throughout the world, which, again, I believe to be certain even though its progress may be irregular.

It is hardly surprising, in view of their characteristics, that Soviet Russia should in her new tactic of coexistence concentrate upon these territories. They clearly offer an exceptionally favorable field for the expansion of communist power by nonmilitary means. Undoubtedly, the emphasis placed by the Russians in the new coexistence era is upon propaganda, diplomacy, economic penetration, rather than direct military assault. This is what they mean by "competitive coexistence": "let the communist countries compete with the capitalist countries in trying to win the allegiance of these uncommitted areas." That is what Khrushchev has said to us. And he has made it quite plain that it certainly is going to be competition. There is so far no question of the Russians giving up their communist ideology or their belief in the ultimate success of world communism.

Nevertheless, before we consider the prospect and problems thrown up by the new Soviet tactics, it is as well to glance for a moment at the purely military problem. After all, the new tactics may be no more than a blind; if the communists so decided, the mask could be dropped and a military offensive let loose very swiftly. Is there, then, in these parts of the world any serious danger of military attack?

If there is such a serious danger, there is no doubt where it is likely to arise. Geography alone indicates two points where an attack from the communist *bloc* would be most probable. The first is in the Middle East, where the attack would come from Russia through Persia or Turkey or conceivably Afghanistan. The second is in South Asia, where it would come from China southwards through Indo-China, Thailand, or Burma.

As far as the Middle East is concerned, there must be considerable temptations to Russia, first because in the Middle East lie very large oil reserves upon which the West is decidedly dependent, and secondly because this historic land bridge between three continents, the cradle of classical civilization, the scene of so many invasions and campaigns, is, for Russia, the gateway to Africa. Therefore, a swift and successful campaign, as a result of which the whole of the territory from the Caspian to the Mediterranean and the Red Sea fell into the hands of Russia, would have enormously significant economic and strategic consequences.

Nevertheless, my conclusion is that such an attack is at present in the highest degree unlikely. It would involve a complete change of front from the policy adopted and openly proclaimed in the last few years. Secondly, even before President Eisenhower's recent statement to Congress, the Western powers had given the Soviet Union a pretty clear warning that they would not tolerate a military assault of this kind without retaliation. In fact, the Russians have been warned that any such onslaught would lead to the Third World War, including full use of thermonuclear weapons. As far as one can see, the Russians have no desire to precipitate such a catastrophe, which, they realize, would be disastrous for themselves as well as for everybody else. The only question is whether they believe the warnings of the West, and for the moment I am inclined to think that they do.

Thirdly, in this Middle East area the Russians have every reason for believing that the prospects of internal revolution are exceedingly good. In most of these countries wealth and power are concentrated in the hands of a small class while the mass of the people live in appalling poverty. At the same time the growth of education is beginning to provide leadership for the potential revolutionary forces. Furthermore, there is the major irritant of Arab-Israel relations to encourage a fanatical nationalism. In balancing the relative advantages of military action or civil penetration, the Russians must give very heavy weight to all this.

Finally, it is not unlikely that their experience in Hungary will make them hesitate before committing themselves to military occupation of any more foreign countries. Although Arab nationalism is a force which at present they can make use of against the West, they probably appreciate the danger that, if they themselves were to become the dominant imperialist power, this force would be turned against them.

For these reasons, I conclude that a military attack through the Middle East is very unlikely at present. Nevertheless, it would be foolish to dismiss it altogether and permanently, and it is certainly necessary that adequate deterrents should exist to discourage any ideas of this kind.

It is also possible that the Chinese may from time to time favor the idea of expanding southwards. Nevertheless, I do not believe a military attack in the near future is likely in this part of the world either. Certainly, there is no sign of it; nor indeed can one say that since the Chinese communist revolution there is much evidence that the new regime is anxious to increase the area it controls by military means. There are grounds for believing that even in the case of Korea the Chinese intervened chiefly because they were frightened of attack. It is of some significance that they have refrained from attacking the off-shore islands of Quemoy and Matsu, though this may be due to warnings from the United States. Similar warnings against the launching of an attack southwards must also deter them. They must surely reckon on retaliation in some form — for instance, if they were to invade Thailand — though admittedly this would not be an easy situation for the West to handle.

The part the Chinese played at the Bandoeng Conference does not suggest that they are thinking of a war of aggression in Asia. They made great efforts to convince the delegates of their honest belief in coexistence. They supported and sponsored resolutions which in some ways were highly critical of Soviet policy, because of their desire for agreement with the other countries represented there.

They too may well feel that expansion involving government by the Chinese of countries which are racially different would cause more trouble than it is worth. Certainly in Burma and Malaya there are substantial Chinese minorities, but the very presence of

these minorities gives some idea of the racial conflicts which could develop if the Chinese were to
gain control of them. The situation in these territories might in time become similar to that now
developing in Central and Eastern Europe in relation to Russia.

The comparison fits in another way. It cannot be
assumed that local communist parties would necessarily remain under the full control of the Chinese.
For instance, in Indo-China Ho Chi Minh might well
take an independent line. Finally, the Chinese people feel, like the Russians, that they have a good prospect of success by propaganda and example. At the
moment they appear very confident of the economic
achievements which are on the way and of the effect
which these may have on the peoples of South and
Southeast Asia.

If, then, the danger of aggression is slight, it may
be asked whether the alliances which have been
formed both in the Middle and Far East as part of
the policy of containing communism are worthwhile.

In earlier lectures I have made it plain that, in
principle, collective defense pacts are a natural supplement to the United Nations in the present state
of the world. But it would be wrong to conclude
from this that any alliance anywhere is a good thing.
In the case of NATO we have a real alliance, not a
paper alliance, with reasonably clear-cut commit-

ments formed by nations with essentially the same background, aims, and outlook.

In the parts of the world with which we are now concerned, no such conditions exist. There are, on the contrary, fairly serious difficulties which stand in the way of effective defensive alliances.

To begin with, the Western powers suffer in these areas from the taint of "colonialism." And then, an attempt to form alliances may lead to local resentment because the West is said to be dividing one Asian country from another and exploiting local disputes and hostilities. For instance, it is certainly one of the grievances in the Middle East against the Bagdad Pact that it deliberately divides Iraq from the other Arab states. I should add, however, that sometimes these grievances reflect the anger of the most powerful local nation that its own dominance in the area is threatened.

Again, the technical and psychological problems associated with land fighting in Asia can hardly be exaggerated, especially if the local populations are indifferent or even hostile. Nor can we dismiss these difficulties by reliance on nuclear weapons. On the contrary, unless we are prepared to forfeit the good will of Asia entirely, we could only contemplate this if it were necessary to protect an Asian country which was wholeheartedly in the struggle — such as the Philippines. We must not forget that in most of Asia it is still believed that the atom bomb was dropped in Japan and not in Europe because Japan was an Asian country.

Another difficulty is the instability of many of the governments in these territories — instability not in the sense of Western governments, which, though they fall frequently in some countries, are usually followed by broadly similar governments, but instability in a much more fundamental sense.

A great deal turns on the attitude of the local populations as well as their governments. If these are ready and indeed anxious to resist the communist forces, then there is both a much stronger reason for the West to go to their help and much greater hope of success. But it is precisely in such cases that the communists are least likely to attack.

One is driven to the conclusion, therefore, that the political front is the really vital one and that the value of a military alliance itself turns largely on its political consequences. Here there are two distinct and indeed opposite possibilities to be borne in mind. The alliance may give encouragement and confidence to the anticommunist forces and help to check defeatism. On the other hand it may cause so much hostility for the reasons I have given that its political effect is highly damaging. I conclude, therefore, that it is most unwise to generalize about pacts of this kind; it is best to treat each situation on its merits. If we can create successfully areas or bands of collective security in danger spots, well and good; but we should be sure that the pacts are effective before entering into them and that the military and political advantages and disadvantages have been very carefully weighed against each other.

I turn now to the nonmilitary problems in these areas. That the Soviet Union has been making very considerable efforts in the last year or two to secure greater influence in Asia and the Middle East cannot be denied. Her trade with these territories has increased very substantially. Although it is still quite a small proportion of their total trade, nevertheless the skill of the Soviets in offering to buy up surpluses and help countries in this way as soon as they have balance of payments difficulties, together with their willingness to grant substantial credits, could, if it were persisted in, make a substantial impression.

For communism, in the ideological war, starts with considerable advantages in these territories. First, they are all countries which desire to see a higher degree of industrialization and economic planning, planning which it is generally admitted must in such cases be carried out by the government. They have heard spectacular accounts of the success of the Russian economic policy over the past thirty years and particularly the past ten years. They see tremendous positive efforts being made in Russia to expand electric power, steel, and coal production, and to develop heavy engineering. In the typical liberal economies of the West, although there may be, and indeed is, substantial economic progress, it is not associated so directly with governments and it seldom receives the same degree of publicity.

Secondly, it must be remembered that, in India particularly — but to some extent the same would be true of the Middle East — there is less awareness of the dangers of totalitarianism than in the West. Few Indians have any vivid appreciation of the experiences which Europe went through during the time of Hitler, nor do they take very seriously the postwar aggressive activities of Stalin. Europe is for them a rather remote place. The rape of Czechoslovakia had little meaning to a people busily engaged on the exciting business of winning their independence. Recent events in Hungary may make a difference in this respect. And it is a matter of particular satisfaction that the Asian Socialist Congress came down so very firmly against Soviet policy in Hungary, and that the most outspoken Indian politician was the leader of the Socialist Party, who did not hesitate bitterly to criticize Pandit Nehru for the rather equivocal attitude which he first of all adopted.

Thirdly, because these countries are poor and Russia is still poorer than the West, there is some instinctive feeling for Russia as against, say, the United States. Fourthly, the Russians can claim, and with some justification, that they have not pursued policies of racial repression, that they do not believe in color bars, and that in this respect at least they follow the socialist — or, if you wish, liberal — principle of fundamental equality.

But more important than any of these as an influence on the side of communist propaganda is that Russia is not one of the Western imperialist powers which at one time ruled these countries and which still govern substantial colonial empires of their own. The fact that Russia has her own colonial empire in Europe is unfortunately not a sufficient counterweight because, as I have said, it is something of which neither the Indians, nor the Arabs for that matter, take very much cognizance.*

I must spend a little more time on the "anticolonialism" issue. For this has surely now become one of the most significant influences in world affairs. How is one to define it? How is one even to describe it?

One can say it is a feeling of strong resentment, sometimes leading to bitter hatred, felt by millions of Asian and African people against the white races and the powerful Western countries. But what precisely is it that is resented and hated? In the first place, of course, it is direct colonial rule against the wishes of the inhabitants. Algeria is the most obvious example in the minds of the people of the un-

* The government of Iraq is a notable exception.

committed areas today, though the Indians rightly or wrongly also see Goa as a continual irritant, a reminder that Western countries by force continue to exercise power in the East. The resentment, however, is not merely against colonial rule as such, but against powerful nations imposing their will by force upon weaker ones. And there is also resentment against racial superiority. All the behavior and institutions associated with the color bar, for instance, are fuel to the flames of colonialist hatred. Finally, there is resentment against economic inequalities.

One cannot say that it is any one of these four characteristics which should be described as anticolonialism, but when all four are combined, resentment is certainly at its highest. Resentment exists, however, even when not all of these characteristics are present.

For example, the extent of direct colonial rule has enormously diminished. Since the war, the British, French, and Dutch between them have given independence to 600 million people in their onetime colonies. The remaining colonial empires are only a fraction of what they were. Yet this has not led to the disappearance of anticolonialist feelings. Apart from the fact that in Africa, particularly, direct colonial government still remains, memories of past colonial rule are deep and likely to last for a long, long time. It is hardly necessary to emphasize this to an American audience who have probably not forgotten George III!

And even when no direct colonial rule exists, there are "semicolonial" relationships which are resented. For instance, in the Middle East, the British, even after the end of any direct rule, continued to exercise considerable influence through diplomatic representatives and treaties of various kinds, of which the one with Jordan is much the best known. One cannot say this has been very successful. Arab nationalism has been roused against us.

But even a less close contact may provoke resentment. Among the peoples of the uncommitted areas there can be, for instance, quite strong feeling against what they would call dollar imperialism — rich America buying up the power and influence which she wants.

It is a remarkable paradox that in a period when there has been such a vast retreat from imperialism by the West such anticolonialist feelings should have become so greatly intensified. One reason for it is that communications have brought about a greater sense of unity among the colonial and ex-colonial peoples. The Bandoeng Conference was significant, not only because of the principles accepted there, not only because it was a success, but because for the first time the Asian and African peoples came together to form their own particular association and express their own particular grievances.

Faced, then, with these fairly serious disadvantages in trying to retain the good will and friendship of the uncommitted areas for the West and in trying to prevent their domination by the communist bloc, what sort of policies should we follow?

There are small groups in Europe who believe that the policy hitherto adopted by Great Britain and, to some extent also, by Holland and France, of granting independence to the colonial territories, is fundamentally mistaken. Such persons, although not so foolish as to suggest that we ought to retrace our steps, are inclined to resist any proposals for moving farther along the same path. They argue that we should use our power to impose our will upon these peoples, that force is the only thing they recognize, and that in doing so we shall really be helping them because the form of government which we provide for them is far better than anything they can provide for themselves. We shall also, it is argued, by continuing to govern directly ourselves, prevent any danger of direct Soviet control.

I have expressed this crudely, because one cannot really speak of a clear-cut policy here. It is, rather, a collection of strong prejudices which are expressed when particular problems in colonial policy are under discussion. These prejudices tend to be found in an especially strong form when there are multiracial problems in a colony, and, indeed, they are probably held more vehemently by white settlers than by the inhabitants of the mother countries.

In my opinion there is no future whatever for such a point of view. It is evident that the United States of America would not be a party to repressive policies of this kind. That being so, it is extremely doubtful whether the United Kingdom, even if aided by other countries in Western Europe, could on its own provide the necessary power should Soviet Russia be in a position and decide to intervene against the colonial powers. Moreover, these policies gravely underestimate the immense force of nationalist feeling. They also fail to appreciate the advantage which communist propaganda has if it is working together with such nationalist feeling. Finally, if it is hard for the Soviet dictatorship to impose its will on the peoples of Hungary and Poland, despite the use of tanks and terror and all the apparatus of totalitarianism, it is infinitely more difficult — indeed, I would say impossible — for a democracy whose people are brought up to believe in the fundamental rights of man to liberty and self-government to do any such thing. A democracy cannot for long maintain a policy of complete repression in its colonies without the people of that democracy themselves deciding to abandon the struggle. And of course it is not only public opinion at home but public opinion in the rest of the world which will declare itself

against policies of this kind. For, with all the set-
backs and disappointments, there surely can be no
doubt of the growing revulsion in this last half
century against the idea that might is right. This
revulsion is particularly strong in the uncommitted
areas, which in consequence, as I pointed out earlier,
tend to be particularly strong supporters of the
United Nations.

We must, then, reject this out-of-date point of
view which unfortunately crops up from time to
time. On the contrary, if the uncommitted areas are
to stay outside the communist orbit, I am sure we
should push on as fast as we can with the granting
of independence and freedom to the remaining colonial territories. If India today really believed that
Great Britain was not determined on this course,
I doubt if she would remain for long within the
commonwealth. The remarkably friendly relations
which exist today between Britain and her former
Asian dominions are due not only to the fact that we
conceded freedom and independence in time, but
also to the conviction that because we kept our
promises to them we are going to do the same in
respect to other colonial territories. This does not
mean that we are expected to grant self-government
next month or next year to all the African colonies.
The extraordinary difficulties of multiracial societies
are understood by our friends in Asia. But they do expect real progress and a genuine acceptance of the

ultimate objective. We have to give continual reassurance on this point by words and deeds. In this way we shall damp down and, I hope, finally extinguish the anticolonialist resentment and passions which unfortunately linger on. Incidentally, as and when this happens, we may find that the so-called Afro-Asian bloc either becomes much more friendly to the West or ceases to be a bloc.

We should underline the connection between parliamentary democracy and progressive colonial policies. It has always seemed to me that there was a clear logical association here; a people which accepts the basic principle of political equality at home, implicit in universal franchise and free elections, cannot really insist that as a group it is entitled to govern other people. This may take a long time, but sooner or later it is bound to emerge. We should make the connection clear, because it is one of the most powerful arguments against totalitarian communism in a colonial territory; and, of course, we can follow it up by exposing the Russian record in Europe, particularly in the light of what has happened in Hungary in recent weeks.

We should also accept the fact that most of these countries prefer to adopt a neutralist position. This is particularly the case with India. There are various reasons for it, some of which have already been mentioned. It springs in part from anticolonial feelings. Because the Western powers are still regarded as "colonialist," India does not want to be too closely associated with them. It springs often from a lack of understanding of recent European history and a consequent tendency to underestimate the danger of aggression from totalitarian states. It springs also from an unwillingness to commit their countries to heavy defense expenditure when they wish to devote all the energies they can to building up their economies. It springs, above all, from something which Americans more than anybody else will understand — the desire, having secured their independence, to start up on their own without any leading strings and without any ties with their past rulers. In short, they wish to get away from "the wickedness of power politics" in very much the same way as the United States wanted to have as little as possible to do with Europe after the War of Independence.

We should, I suggest, be sympathetic to these attitudes, and we should not press these countries to join alliances if they do not wish to. Incidentally, in adopting neutralist policies, they are probably less likely to be undermined by communist influence than if they were too closely associated with the West and so, contrary to the desires of their people, came to be regarded as "stooges" of Western imperialism.

There remains a question which will probably be in your minds — can we afford to withdraw from these colonial territories, giving them their independence, without risking serious military weakness? Specifically, the question is posed in relation to certain naval and air bases.

Nobody would deny the possibility of a clash between military and political considerations, and no doubt there are cases where it is a matter of balancing the one against the other. But in making up our minds as to what we should do about these bases, there are three points to bear in mind. The bases themselves are not going to be much use if they are surrounded by a hostile population. We must, therefore, seek agreement, if we wish to retain a base, with the local government. Then we have to ask ourselves whether, in the present state of technical development, such bases are really any longer quite so essential as they were a few years ago. Finally, if we do decide to hold them, then we must do everything we can to keep the use of the bases distinct from political control. In this respect, the United States policy of leasing air bases fairly unobtrusively and without political intervention seems a sensible approach to this problem.

This brings me, finally, to the question of economic aid. What is the case for it, and how should it be administered?

The case is clear enough. Although within most advanced industrial countries inequality of living standards between different sections of the population has diminished in recent years, the gap between the average standard of living in poorer and richer countries has probably widened. This in itself is a cause for some alarm, since it may intensify those feelings of resentment to which I referred a few moments ago.

It seems to me we have a situation like this. On the one hand, there are advanced industrial nations who for a long time now have been accustomed to a steady rise in their standard of living as a result of the application of more or less continuous technical progress and a high rate of saving and investment. This is associated, as a rule, with birth control in some form or other so that population increases are kept within bounds. At the other extreme is a group of countries whose people have for centuries done no more than scratch a living and keep themselves alive. Up to now they have not managed to reach the escalator of economic progress. But today, as communications develop and knowledge spreads about what is happening in other countries, new aspirations emerge and there is an increasing demand by these peoples for the opportunities which more advanced countries enjoy. As I said earlier, they look at the communist states and they see the governments there taking the initiative and driving through great programs of economic development. They see that the Russians are already on the escalator of progress; and they are naturally tempted by these examples. Perhaps more important — especially for the Asian countries — they hear of developments in China.

But in order to achieve this economic progress, certain conditions have to be fulfilled. There has to be a higher rate of investment, and, therefore, a higher rate of saving. Many customs have to be altered if productivity is to increase. There has to be a spreading of technical knowledge and "know-how," some of it quite simple, so that the investment in machinery, plant, and equipment can be put to proper use.

These changes can undoubtedly be forced through far more easily by a dictatorship than under democratic conditions. For a dictatorship can use its power — as the Kremlin has — to hold down living standards ruthlessly for the time being and insure that an abnormally high proportion of available resources is devoted to investment or defense rather than to consumption. A democracy is not in the same position to disappoint human hopes and aspirations. Any government elected on a democratic basis has to produce some results fairly quickly if it is to survive. The danger, therefore, is that it will not be prepared sufficiently to sacrifice the present for the future, and that the pace of industrial advance will therefore be too slow.

This is the dilemma which faces a democracy in such conditions. Either it goes too slowly, in which case adverse comparisons will be made with more rapidly advancing communist states; or its progress is fast, in which case the discontent created by holding down the rate of consumption may result in an explosion and provide just the conditions in which the communists come into power.

There is only one way out of the dilemma. If these countries are both to make rapid economic progress and to retain their democratic systems, they must be given some outside help. I believe that upon the possibility of this help turns more than on anything else the question of whether they stay democratic.

Before discussing the ways and means of economic help, I must make it plain that economic development, with or without aid, is no alternative to political freedom, for countries which are still colonies. On the contrary, we have to face the fact that in such countries economic progress, and particularly the better education of the people, is likely to create rather than solve political problems. This is something which cannot be avoided, for if there is to be economic development, there must be more education, and if there is to be more education, then there will be more demands for political freedom. The alternative of leaving these countries to stagnate, even if it were ethically tolerable, is no solution, because the spread of ideas from outside areas is inevitable with modern communications and in time would probably produce an even bigger explosion. Even in countries which are already independent, a somewhat similar problem arises, where the whole process will stimulate the demand for more rapidly rising living standards. This can be beneficial rather than dangerous, providing it is linked with an understanding of the necessary conditions of progress and an emotional enthusiasm for development.

As to the form of the outside assistance, I have only a few obvious comments to make on a subject on which a great deal of work has already been done. Indeed, I would go so far as to say that the problems of this work are no longer technical but political. The experts are mostly in agreement about what should be done; the question is whether the politicians and the people will do it.

I do not think that anybody can seriously expect private investment to do the job. There are many reasons why it has not in fact been able to do so up to now, and these reasons are likely to continue. In some cases, there is doubt about the stability of the government and of the local currency. In other cases, there is fear of opposition to foreign capital or of unfair fiscal treatment. Then the yield on investments at home has been so high recently that there is no great incentive for private individuals or corporations to invest abroad.

There are, of course, some exceptions. There are the extractive industries, where the need to secure supplies of raw materials provides special incentives. There is also investment more or less forced upon a foreign company because of high tariffs or other protective controls.

But apart from cases of this kind, the basic capital formation in these countries will, in the main, have to be undertaken by the governments. We would be foolish to allow any prejudice against "socialist" projects to influence our judgment in this matter. It is not, and certainly should not be, the object of the exercise to try and spread the theory and practice of economic liberalism. Indeed, I have for long thought that the confusion between political democracy and a laissez-faire economic policy was one of the most unfortunate and dangerous fallacies — which, however well intentioned its authors may be, has done much harm to the solidarity of the free world.

Moreover, there is an obvious danger that a reliance on private foreign investment — especially in the early stages — would result in strong antagonisms developing against "dollar imperialism," though I hasten to add that many international companies have through experience become highly skilled nowadays in handling their relationships with foreign governments and peoples.

Secondly, it is highly desirable that the initiative for foreign loans or foreign aid, as for the whole development of the countries concerned, should as far as possible come from within. For countries which are already self-governing, or soon will be, should learn to manage their own affairs; and, if they do, there will be much less friction with the outside world. One reason for the success of the Colombo Plan is that the Asian countries which participate have each worked out their own development plans, though they came together with each other and with friends from the West to discuss these plans and to give each other advice and help. The Western countries who are members have been — as it were — at the disposal of the Asian countries, ready to provide technical help and fairly small amounts of direct finance.

Thirdly, any aid, whether in the form of grants or loans, should be without military strings. Any attempt to associate this aid with direct military conditions or, still more, with defense contributions, would be a mistake. It is likely to be refused, and even if it is not refused, will probably sow the seeds of future trouble. Nor is it wise that economic help should be concentrated simply on those territories where the danger of communism is said to be greatest. For, if this course were to be followed, then the West would lay itself open to continuous blackmail.

The problem is admittedly a delicate one. It would be dangerous to give the impression that the countries supplying capital are simply making use of the underdeveloped areas for their own strategic ends. But equally, it would be wrong to treat the whole business as an act of charity for which gratitude is expected. Few relationships are more unsatisfactory than that of rich uncle — poor nephew. So the path of the idealistic Westerner is admittedly difficult! I think the answer is that the aid should be provided for the sole purpose of enabling economic development to take place faster and more smoothly in a stable democratic society; and that the whole transaction should be based on this principle. Any conditions, supervision, or guidance should be linked to this and to this alone.

Even so, the relationship is not going to be an easy one. In my opinion there will be less friction if the aid is channeled through international institutions. One of the outstanding successes of the postwar period has been the work of the International Bank, which unobtrusively and efficiently has advanced substantial sums of money to countries almost all over the world. I do not believe this could have been done even by the United States on its own without creating far more friction in its relations with the uncommitted territories.

I would myself go further. I am already on record as favoring in principle the SUNFED proposals, which have been discussed so often at the United Nations. I believe that a big gesture of this kind would help relations between the uncommitted areas and the West partly because, if international aid is channeled through the United Nations, there is less opportunity for the Russians to make political capital. In fact, either the Russians would have to make their contribution in that way, which would deprive them of the opportunity of linking it with communist propaganda, or, if they refused to join, they would be exposed as providing aid only in order to achieve influence.

It may be said that the United Nations is not yet organized for this work. That is, no doubt, true, but there is no reason why there should not be a gradual expansion. The necessary staffs could be built up, the necessary experience obtained. The essential point is to make a start with a plan, perhaps on the modest lines already suggested in the SUNFED proposals, but moving on to rather more ambitious projects. I am certainly not going to commit myself to a definite figure. But it is interesting that a number of different investigations seem to settle on a figure of something like three to four billion dollars a year as that which it should be within the capacity of the underdeveloped countries to absorb.

I have now come to the end of my analysis of these three spheres in which the problem of coexistence presents itself: the United Nations, Europe, and the uncommitted areas, and I must try to pull the threads together. If I were asked to single out the most important themes which I have tried to develop, they would be these.

First, the Charter of the United Nations, although suffering from various drawbacks, is nevertheless a code of conduct which democratic, peace-loving states should observe.

Secondly, however, the Charter cannot cover every situation, nor can we rely upon the United Nations Organization on its own to provide full collective security against aggression. It therefore follows that our support for the United Nations must be accompanied by a clear understanding of its inevitable limitations. While trying to strengthen it, we must not regard those limitations as an excuse for avoiding a positive foreign policy alongside of and as a supplement to working through the United Nations. *Thirdly,* it is still necessary that the Atlantic Alliance should be sustained and encouraged. This requires not only closer co-operation on specific European problems but also a genuine readiness to consult on issues arising in other parts of the world affecting the interests of the member countries of NATO. Such closer consultation and co-operation does not, however, mean that we should follow rigid or tough foreign policies all the time. On the contrary, recent developments suggest that a more flexible policy may bring important results. But the policy is something which should be worked out together and not decided by any one government on its own.

Further, we should recognize the great significance of our relationships with the underdeveloped countries — both by word and in deed. We should continue to make plain our determination to abide by democratic principles and to assist and foster the development of self-government and independence in former colonies. We should bear in mind the intense feelings which, partly for historic reasons, surround the word "colonialism," and we should so conduct ourselves as to minimize friction arising therefrom.

We should recognize too the need for giving economic help to these underdeveloped countries and to do so without expecting a flood of appreciation or attaching to such help any military strings. We should always bear in mind that our sole objective in helping them is that they may move into a position where they can enjoy the same opportunities of economic progress as we in the West have enjoyed for many years and do this on a stable and democratic basis.

It so happens that almost all these themes in a strange way converge together in the complex problem of the Middle East. A study of events there in recent years, and particularly in recent weeks, shows them in their different ways, one by one. So I think it would be appropriate if, at the very end of these talks, I were to say a few words about this part of the world, not in order to describe in detail developments which have taken place there, but rather to illustrate the conclusions which I have been trying to draw for policy as a whole.

First, then, let us look at the Middle East question

from the point of view of the United Nations. Here was a case where the United Nations can be said to have had in the last five years at least a partial success. The observers now working under General Burns were not able to stop the frontier incidents, but nobody would say that they were without some influence, nor did anybody propose seriously that the United Nations should cease to care for the number of Arab refugees in Jordan and Egypt. But it must be admitted that the success was a very partial one, even if the problem was the most profound and difficult one existing in the world today.

Then came the nationalization of the canal. For nearly three months negotiations and discussions of one kind or another took place on this subject. Although it was weeks before the Security Council was formally appraised of the dispute, there was nothing in this contrary to the charter. Although its deliberations on the matter did not result in agreement, some progress was made and at least up to the end of October the threat of open armed conflict had been averted.

Then followed the attack by Israel upon Egypt on October 29. I would not say that this was an entirely straightforward issue. There is reason to believe that provocation existed. In the ordinary way, it was a matter which should clearly have been handled by the Security Council, with a view not only to obtaining a cease fire and the withdrawal of Israeli forces within existing frontiers, but also to dealing with the root causes of the conflict and the threats to the security of Israel.

The question, however, could not be dealt with simply on these lines, because of the decision of the British and French to issue on their own their ultimatum of October 30. This ultimatum and the action which followed were regarded by the overwhelming majority of the members of the United Nations as, in effect, a violation of the charter. It was also so regarded by a large body of opinion within Great Britain itself. The Assembly, therefore, was in this case certainly registering world opinion; it was, in doing so, successful in inducing the British and French governments first to agree to a cease fire and later to withdraw their forces from Egypt.

Let us recognize this as an initial success for the principles of the charter and indeed for the institutions of the United Nations. But let us also give credit to the two great democracies who, because they were democracies, decided to bow to world opinion. We cannot but contrast their behavior with the very different conduct of Soviet Russia in ignoring the repeated requests of the United Nations Assembly in relation to Hungary.

We should have no illusions, however. This initial success will quickly disappear, if that is all the United Nations is able to do in the Middle East.

There exist today three problems which must be

faced. First, the Suez Canal has to be cleared as fast as possible. Secondly, there must be a settlement of the future control of the canal. Thirdly, a great effort must be made to improve relations and ultimately settle the dispute between Israel and the Arab states.

As far as the clearance of the canal is concerned, the United Nations are themselves doing the necessary technical job. The only difficulty that appears to exist at present is a political one. Let us hope that it will melt away. But it would be quite wrong for the United Nations to tolerate from Egypt any intention to obstruct the clearance of the canal in order to obtain political advantages elsewhere.

Then, as regards the control of the canal, there are three things that must be said. First, negotiations should be resumed as soon as possible at the point where they were broken off at the end of October. A solution acceptable to both Egypt and the canal users was, I believe, not far off. The details are covered in the letter of the Secretary General to the Egyptian Foreign Minister. Secondly, it would be most unsatisfactory if in this settlement the Egyptian government were still left free to refuse the passage of Israeli ships. That would be to condone a continuing civil wrong; for it is not reasonable that Israel should be put in the position that, in regard to free passage through the canal, it is supposed to be in a state of war with Egypt, but in regard to the use of force on its own frontiers, then, apparently, it must behave as if it were at peace. So on this matter, too, the United Nations should stand firm against any Egyptian objections. Thirdly, any idea that the free passage of British and French ships should be linked with the withdrawal of Israeli forces must be firmly resisted. Colonel Nasser has repeatedly promised that there will be no discrimination when Egypt operates the canal. He must be held to this promise.

I cannot emphasize too strongly the painful impression which will be created in Britain if, after the strong pressures brought upon Britain and France and Israel to accept the resolutions of the Assembly, the United Nations now proceed to show weakness or timidity in the face of obstruction on the part of Egypt. Precisely because in my party we opposed the action of the British and French governments, we feel entitled to underline this point. Were this to happen, there would develop in Europe a growing cynicism and indifference toward the United Nations and, let me be frank, a growing irritation with the policies of the United States.

You may say, "But how can the United Nations insist on getting its way if Egypt proves adamant?" And, "How can we be sure that the United Nations Assembly itself agrees to the course proposed?"

On the assumption that a clear two-thirds majority is available, then it surely would be the duty of the United States and other powers who take the lead in this matter, to bring pressures to bear in order to secure that the decisions of the Assembly are observed. But even supposing no great majority exists, then this cannot absolve great powers with responsibilities such as those carried by the United States from any further action. Here we have a case where we may well come up against the limit of what the United Nations can do. You will recall that in my first lecture I was at pains to emphasize that there was such a limit. When we reach that limit, it simply means that other channels and other methods — not in conflict with the charter, though outside the Assembly — may have to be used. I repeat that weakness in this field could be dangerous not only for the reputation of the United Nations but also for the Atlantic Alliance.

The third problem — that of Israel-Arab relations — is far more difficult. And I do not propose tonight to attempt to outline the solution. But I will say this. The problem in my opinion is not so much one of establishing what would be a reasonable settlement in the long run. It is not difficult to set out the various steps that would have to be taken, the various headings of any ultimate agreement. The problem here at the moment is essentially psychological. The passionate feelings of the Arab peoples probably make impossible for the time being any substantial progress toward settlement. Therefore, the first important thing is to gain time, to gain time without armed conflicts so as to allow passions to subside.

That is one reason why I, myself, favor the proposal that not only the Gaza Strip, but a corridor of territory running from Gaza to the Gulf of Aqaba along the Egyptian-Israeli frontier, should be taken over by the United Nations force and, indeed, administered by the United Nations itself. For this would provide a firm barrier against the resumption of attacks on Israel by Egypt or vice versa, and thus, at least, sterilize one frontier. I will go further. I believe that serious consideration should now be given to the possibility of the United Nations Force's being used to patrol not only the borders of Egypt and Israel, but those of Israel with the other Arab states also. If these proposals could be carried through the United Nations Assembly, they would mark a decisive advance toward settlement in the Middle East. But this will only be possible if they are backed by the most powerful country among the Western democracies.

Finally, let me add just this. I recognize that in present circumstances it is perhaps necessary, in relation to matters in the Middle East, for the United States to proceed without close and obvious co-operation with Britain and France. That may be for the moment the better course diplomatically. I would, however, ask very seriously that at least the minimum of consultation with us should take place, and that it should be recognized that, as soon as possible, much closer co-operation will be restored. This carries with it certain implications about the significance of the Suez episode for the future.

First, I would ask that we do not allow any alleged disagreement about "colonialism" to divide us. It is all to the good that the United States should develop closer relations with the countries of Asia and Africa. But let this be for its own sake, and not because of differences on colonial policy. Recall, if you please, the record of Great Britain since the war in granting independence to former colonies and dominions. Remember that this process has not stopped, that in March of this year Ghana achieves independence, that it is expected that within the next few years this will be followed by Nigeria, Malaya, and the West Indies. Do not forget that France, too, has moved along the same path, in Indo-China, Tunis, and Morocco. Please understand that millions of British people are very proud of these changes and of the new emerging free commonwealth, whose unity depends on an acceptance of the ideals behind them. In view of all this, would it not seem a little absurd for America to appear to cut herself off from Britain because Britain was still pursuing colonialist ideas? Since the fateful decision to accept the cease fire, I am glad to say that the British government seems to be moving back again toward the policy of friendship with America, commonwealth unity, and respect for the United Nations. Although we in the Labor Party have strongly opposed particular measures pursued in particular colonies by the British government — Cyprus is the most recent example — as a serious, realistic policy for Britain, "colonialism" is dead and can never be revived.

You will see from this that I do not share the views of those observers who are drawing all sorts of conclusions about decisive changes in British foreign policy in consequence of the Suez episode, who are now discovering that this has its roots in all sorts of fundamental divisions among the Western powers, which in time were bound to produce last autumn's harvest. For my part I look on the Suez episode as a temporary affair, an aberration which, to be sure, leaves behind a formidable host of problems, but which should not lead us away from old friendships and ideals. It would be a great tragedy if at this moment it were to be accepted by the statesmen who govern our countries that what has happened had created a great and irreparable breach between America and Europe.

For surely what has happened in Eastern Europe gives us, the people of the democracies, the greatest hope and encouragement that we have had for these past ten years. It shows that, however many mistakes the democracies make, whatever their weaknesses may be, the ideals of political freedom and self-government are ideals still cherished by the peoples living in the communist countries, whereas the dogmas of totalitarian communism are rejected and detested by them. One cannot help recalling Stalin's famous question in one of the wartime discussions — "How many divisions has the Pope?" I am not a Catholic, but, in a metaphorical sense I would answer "Quite a lot." Hungary has shown that. The spirit of man has not been conquered.

These ideals of ours are also substantially those which the people in the uncommitted areas, particularly in India, accept. There is nothing surprising about this, for the ideals have owed much in turn to the United States in the ringing phrases of the Declaration of Independence, to France in the stirring battle cries of the French Revolution, and to Britain through her long experience of parliamentary democracy. We now know that tyranny will not crush the passion for liberty, that "government of the people, by the people, for the people" is still the greatest and most influential political concept of all time. This, surely, should encourage our two nations not to part company, but rather to pursue our common struggle with all the greater faith and courage.

H 3